A Room with a View

A Room
with a View

*Ministry with
the world at your door*

NICHOLAS HOLTAM

First published in Great Britain in 2008

Society for Promoting Christian Knowledge
36 Causton Street
London SW1P 4ST

British Library Cataloguing-in-Publication Data
A catalogue record for this book is available from the British Library

ISBN 978–0–281–05967–6

1 3 5 7 9 10 8 6 4 2

Designed and typeset by Kenneth Burnley, Wirral, Cheshire.
Printed in Great Britain by Ashford Colour Press

Produced on paper from sustainable forests

Contents

A poem for St Martin-in-the-Fields,
part of which is inscribed
on the handrail of the
light-well in Church Path

Now traveller, whose journey passes through
Tall courts of shifting light, and trudging crowds
Continually worn down but always new,

Your stepping inwards from the air to earth
Winds round itself to meet the open sky
So vanishing becomes a second birth.

Fare well. Return. Fare well. Return again.
Here home and elsewhere share one mystery.
Here love and conscience sing the same refrain.
Here time leaps up. And strikes eternity.

Andrew Motion

Acknowledgements

I am enormously grateful to my colleagues and the team of people who have been responsible for the renewal of St Martin's. There really are too many to name, partly because it has been a big project and also because it has taken 11 years! We worked out quite early on that one of my responsibilities as Vicar was to articulate the story of St Martin's. Most of the material in this book has been given in one form or another at St Martin's. I have gained a great deal from being part of that community but am especially indebted to my clergy colleagues, at present Paul Lau, Richard Carter, Liz Russell and Liz Griffiths.

I do not take the St Martin's community for granted in saying that I once asked one of my colleagues where he got his support. Quick as a flash he replied, 'California'. When you are with a community day in, day out, few say that you are doing a good job. Visitors do – and so, sometimes, do the places that invite you to visit them. I am grateful to the churches and cathedrals that invited me to preach, including in the final stage of producing this book Grace Cathedral in San Francisco. The Anglican clergy of Hong Kong, the Diocese of the Highveld in South Africa, and, closer to home, of Salisbury and Worcester have also provided some very engaging and encouraging occasions in which to think and speak about ministry and mission.

The title of this book is E. M. Forster's. It was fun to discover fundraising for the church within that novel but it is the image that works so well for what a parish church aspires to be.

Acknowledgements

Chapter 1 is a slightly revised version of the Eric Abbott Lecture given at Westminster Abbey and Keble College Oxford in 2005. In addition to the clergy at St Martin's, the Very Revd Dr Wesley Carr, formerly Dean of Westminster Abbey, and Revd Dr Richard Burridge, Dean of King's College London, were encouraging readers of a draft. Both have been very good neighbours. Colleagues at the Grubb Institute helped refine it.

Chapter 2 is a revision of a lecture in 2004 at Gresham College, London, versions of which were published in the *Church Times* and in *Justice Reflections*. Colin Glover, Chief Executive of The Connection at St Martin's, helpfully commented on a draft. Will Morris gave a stringent critique.

People come to St Martin's from all over the world. Our architect, James Gibbs, timed his *Book of Architecture* perfectly. It travelled in the 1730s to the colonies. In North America, particularly New England, the absurd and much criticized confusion of architectural styles in which a soaring steeple cut through a classical portico became a model church. There are hundreds of architectural copies of St Martin's in the United States and we now have something of a copyright claim. Setting up a US Foundation for St Martin-in-the-Fields London (there are over 20 St Martin-in-the-Fields in the US) meant finding trustees, the President of whom, Tom Joyce, introduced me to his university, St John's in Collegeville, Minnesota. Chapter 3 started life there and was revised for the Bernard Gilpin Lecture in Pastoral Theology at Durham University in 2006.

Becoming a Curate in Stepney in 1979 meant I had to come to terms with Christianity and other faiths. I won a competition with an essay on the saying of Jesus in John's Gospel that 'No-one comes to the Father except by me', published in *Christian* (Volume 6, Number 3, 1981, pp. 20ff.). After a sabbatical in 1998, the same journal published a sermon on 'Christ our story of stories' (*Christian*, 1998/4, pp. 13ff.). As for many people working in this area, the second of these articles owed a great debt to the late Canon Roger Hooker. Chapter 4 has grown out of these earlier attempts to position myself. I am indebted to Mike and Ruth Wooldridge for their hospitality in India, but also for pointing me to the ashram at Sevagram.

Living and working across the road from the National Gallery is a joy. Chapter 5 comes from that neighbourly relationship. The non-biblical addendum was inspired by Revd John Miller, a former Moderator of the Church of Scotland.

Archbishop Michael Ramsey, who delighted to describe himself as 'sometime Sub-Warden of Lincoln Theological College', where from 1983 to 1987 I was Lecturer in Christian Ethics, said that staff at theological colleges divide into those who hated having to teach across a wide range of subjects beyond their academic competence and interests and those who loved it. By and large I loved it and learnt far more than my students could ever have done. Chapter 6 owes a debt to Lincoln, to two of my own teachers, the late Revd Professor Canon G. R. Dunstan of King's College London and Professor Ann Loades of Durham University, to the people of the parishes where I have ministered, in Stepney, St Michael on the Mount, Lincoln and the Isle of Dogs, as well as St Martin's and to InclusiveChurch.net, especially Savi Hensman and Giles Goddard for ideas that have become my own.

St Martin's has a unique relationship with the BBC and the history of religious broadcasting. It continues in the present day and I am grateful for permission to reproduce the Prayer for the Day in Chapter 10, broadcast on BBC Radio 4, 24 October 2007.

The then Poet Laureate, Cecil and Mrs Jill Day-Lewis, were close friends of my predecessor but one at St Martin's, Prebendary Austen and Daphne Williams. They were, and Jill still is, great supporters of St Martin's. Because of that close association, Jill very generously agreed to my reproducing in full her late husband's poem 'Final Instructions'.

R. S. Thomas was a parish priest and poet. In 2007 his

Acknowledgements

'Emerging' provided the theme for Lent at St Martin's, 'The scaffolding of the spirit'. It is quoted with permission.

Michael Goulder's poem about the genealogy of Matthew comes from his *Midrash and Lection in Matthew* and is reproduced with permission.

Andrew Motion, the Poet Laureate, wrote a poem, two verses of which have been inscribed on the handrail of the new lightwell in what is known as 'Church Path' between the church and the Nash terrace to its north. The poem engages the passer-by with St Martin's and I am grateful he has agreed to it being reprinted here where I hope it will do similar.

The picture on the cover is based on an image of Trafalgar Square by Nigel Young/Foster and Partners and is reproduced with their permission.

Ruth McCurry of SPCK was the Rector's wife when I was a Curate in Stepney. Her friendship, patience and persistence has at last got me to publish.

In some ways this is quite a personal book. Certainly it is *my* view of things but, as Africans seem to know more strongly than the rest of us, 'a person is a person through a person'. I could not have written without the support of members of St Martin's, colleagues, friends and, above all, family. I am grateful to all those who have shared their experiences, perceptions and thoughts and helped me to find myself in the role of the Vicar of St Martin-in-the-Fields.

Introduction

One could not learn history from architecture any more than one could learn it from books. Statues, inscriptions, memorial stones, the names of streets – anything that might throw light upon the past had been systematically altered.

'I never knew it had been a church,' he said.

'There's a lot of them left, really,' said the old man, 'though they've been put to other uses. Now how did that rhyme go? Ah, I've got it!

Oranges and lemons, say the bells of St Clement's,
You owe me three farthings, say the bells of St Martin's.

There now, that's as far as I can get. A farthing, that was a small copper coin, looked something like a cent.'

'Where was St Martin's?' said Winston.

'St Martin's? That's still standing. It's in Victory Square alongside the picture gallery. A building with a kind of triangular porch and pillars in front, and a big flight of steps.'

Winston knew the place well. It was a museum used for propaganda displays of various kinds – scale models of rocket bombs and Floating Fortresses, waxwork tableaux illustrating enemy atrocities, and the like.

'St Martin's-in-the-Fields it used to be called,' supplemented the old man, 'though I don't recollect any fields in those parts.'

(George Orwell, *Nineteen Eighty-Four*)

St Martin-in-the-Fields has got under Britain's skin to an unusual degree. In George Orwell's vision of the future in *Nineteen Eighty-Four*, St Martin's represented a half memory of life as it had been – good, true, human. In *England's Thousand Best Churches* Simon Jenkins, the former editor of *The Times*, said St Martin-in-the-Fields is 'England's most loved, most imitated, most photographed parish church'. Inexplicably, he only gave it three stars out of a possible five, probably because St Martin's looked so worn out. According to the Bishop of London in 1996, St Martin's 'is like the Salvation Army: we all think well of you but none of us has the slightest idea what you really do'. After walking round the buildings in 1997, Neil MacGregor, a neighbour to St Martin's when Director of the National Gallery, exclaimed, 'I had no idea how extensive the buildings were, nor how awful,' helpfully adding, 'Something must be done, and quickly.'

Eleven years isn't that quick but the renewal of St Martin-in-the-Fields is near complete and on a scale most of us never get to think about, let alone do. It has taken an enormous amount of faith and effort on the part of a very large and highly committed team to deliver Eric Parry Architects' plan. Many of the people involved in this project have been inspiring and are world class in their own professional fields. So are the people who day by day are St Martin's.

When we began, there were those who thought we had taken on too much, or that our plans were too expensive. Now we have finished, the common response is that £36 million has been very well spent. The renewed buildings equip St Martin's for service in the twenty-first century.

When we started to talk, analyse and plan there was concern that this work would be an enormous diversion from the main tasks of a church. It has not been so. Indeed, it has intensified our self-understanding and sense of purpose as we worked out why we are there and what we are for. The Parochial Church

Council determined that we would use this opportunity to be renewed as a church – people as well as buildings. It has been an invigorating time.

The world sets the agenda for all serious theology. Parish churches minister not to themselves but to the whole parish and in a context. In the face of Orwell's grim vision of the future, including St Martin's becoming a museum for propaganda and war, the renewal of this much loved church is a significant triumph of Christian determination and spiritual imagination over the destructive possibilities of secularization.

In the Church at large we have got into such a state about declining numbers that 'mission' is the order of the day and 'ministry' is associated with a failing programme of ecclesiastical maintenance. I just don't get it. The pastoral care of individuals and communities connects them with the worship and community life of the Church. Good ministry is about being with people to witness to God's presence and work in the world. Sometimes this is done by clergy. More often it is done through the hundreds of acts of kindness shown by 'ordinary' lay people living out their Christian commitment. In the thirteenth century, when St Francis sent out his brothers to preach the good news of Jesus everywhere, he told them, 'Use words if you have to.'

'Mission' is perceived to be active, yet the location of an architecturally fine church is an enduring witness to the presence of God among us. Of course the building has to point beyond itself to God for this to be effective. I once overheard someone on their mobile phone outside St Martin's saying that they were 'by the clock tower'. So the building *of itself* is not what a church is about. Even so, for millions of people the building speaks of Christ. That is one reason why we have put such energy into its renewal so that St Martin's can continue to speak well of Christ in the heart of London.

Since the 1990s and what was called the 'Decade of Evangelism', the Church of England has got stuck on the idea of 'mission' as meaning evangelism. But mission is really about looking for what God is doing in the world and joining in. There are so many ways of doing this. According to St Paul, the diverse gifts given by the risen and ascended Christ to his disciples were, 'That some would be apostles, some prophets, some evangelists, some pastors and teachers, to equip the saints for the work of ministry, for building up the body of Christ, until all of us come to the unity of the faith and of the knowledge of the Son of God, to maturity, to the measure of the full stature of Christ' (Ephesians 4.11–13)

Good ministry matures and deepens people into the Godly humanity of Jesus Christ.

In December 2007 Channel 5 broadcast three documentaries about St Martin's, 'The parish church of England'. They were a vivid portrayal of a varied and interesting community in which St Martin's was described as 'anything but traditional'. You have to be careful with that sort of language in the Anglican Church nowadays. St Martin's is in fact *very* traditional, what in previous times could have been described as 'Anglican mainstream'. It represents a classical form of Anglicanism – practical, Godly, sensible.

The various parts of St Martin's are good, but the mix is electrifying. It is local *and* international, charitable *and* commercial, open to everyone *and* aspires to excellence. St Martin's has a remarkable ability to handle paradox creatively. It is the Royal parish church *and* the church of the homeless, the Admiralty's parish church *and* the church associated with the founding of the British pacifist movement, the Peace Pledge Union. It is Christian *and* inclusive. It likes to do things well and recognizes that on this side of the kingdom of heaven nearly all ministry is imperfect as well as multifaceted, fragmentary and momentary. Inevitably we make mistakes but, as Bishop John V. Taylor used to say, we hope that our mistakes are made in the right direction.

I have sometimes worried about how to be the Vicar of a

church through a period of such major change. For the last few years I have had to concentrate on fundraising. What started as a strain became at first bearable and then enjoyable as I realized that people would not give for this project to me as a fundraiser and I needed to find a new aspect of being the Vicar. So if you have picked up this book in the hope that it will teach you how to raise £36 million, or how to organize your church for a major buildings project, you are going to be disappointed. Instead, what you are holding is a book about the life of a church in a period of change. What became clear at St Martin's is that we had to be ourselves and we had to take the trouble to find out what that meant and articulate it for ourselves and for others.

So this book comes out of a period of renewal at St Martin-in-the-Fields, not just the physical renewal of buildings but the renewal of ministry in a parish church that has the world at its door. Of course St Martin's is on a scale, in a location and with a history that is unique. Not everything that belongs there belongs everywhere, but some of our experience is common and worth sharing. The pattern of ministry from this particular 'room with a view' will be useful to others.

The Church of England has an elegant statement that has to be read at the beginning of a new ministry. It is the Preface to the Declaration of Assent to be made by the minister.

> The Church of England is part of the One, Holy, Catholic and Apostolic Church, worshipping the one true God, Father, Son and Holy Spirit. It professes the faith uniquely revealed in the Holy Scriptures and set forth in the catholic creeds, *which faith the Church is called upon to proclaim afresh in each generation.* Led by the Holy Spirit, it has borne witness to Christian truth in its historic formularies, the Thirty-nine Articles of Religion, The Book of Common Prayer and the Ordering of Bishops, Priests and Deacons. In the declaration you are about to make, will you affirm

your loyalty to this inheritance of faith as your inspiration and guidance under God in bringing the grace and truth of Christ to this generation and making Him known to those in your care?

St Martin's values standing in that historic tradition and we try to do so creatively. It is a courageous church capable of exercising leadership and breaking new ground. In my first year as Vicar, I asked the Parochial Church Council to give office space to a new organization working on spirituality with gay people in Soho. I expected a difficult discussion. One of the older members of the Council, not someone I would have thought instinctively sympathetic to this particular cause, said, 'That's the sort of thing St Martin's has always done.' A churchwarden agreed and the Council voted unanimously in favour. The willingness to engage with the issues of the day and explore them in faith are marked characteristics of this church.

The only churches worth joining are those that join their members to God in Christ, 'who was reconciling the world to himself'. Christian ministry is not primarily about ecclesiastical minutiae but the relationship between God's kingdom and the world. It is to that the Church is called to bear witness, and it is what this book is about.

CHAPTER 1

A room with a view:
the aspiration of a parish church

A room with a view

The metaphor of 'A room with a view' in relation to an English parish church is intended to suggest three things that are historically and theologically important characteristics currently under threat in the Church of England.

First, it suggests that parish churches should be open to the world. This is a sound instinct about places of prayer. The Talmud advises we should 'never pray in a room without windows'.[1] The question facing every church congregation is whether they save people *from* the world or *in* the world: whether they face inward or outward. My sense is that a great deal of what passes for 'mission' in the contemporary Church of England is peculiarly inward looking. For the last 20 years we have been presented with a false polarity that gives priority to 'mission' over that sort of pastoral care in which ministers and churches cared for the whole parish and not just for the congregation. It is difficult to know cause and effect, but in our anxiety to survive we are creating inward-looking, self-referential congregations. What is needed is churches that help people move between church and world in such a way that they and their world are transformed.[2]

This is particularly important when we have difficulty discerning good religion from bad – and bad religion has assumed lethal potency. The experience of creating public liturgy in response to acts of terrorism has reinforced my belief that our

1

religious life must be shaped and informed by God-given reason as well as the particularities of scripture and Church tradition and teaching. We may well be frightened by some aspects of the world, but it is made by God and is fundamentally good. As Christians we are schooled in it and open to meeting God in it, and to this the Church bears witness. So a parish church must be open to the world and not just set apart from it.

Second, a room that is a place of prayer should be open to the poorest. This matters, or ought to matter, to Christians because of Christ's teaching about God, and the things of God, being known in and among the poor. The Church of England gets muddled about whether we are *for* the poor, *with* the poor, or *of* the poor, but one of the things that persistently undermines our pretension and opens us to God is the possibility that we will meet Christ in the poor. The 'great soul' Gandhi taught that the place of prayer should be a spacious ground under the open sky available to the poorest of the poor. This is about being open to God's world *and* to the poor. It is not far from Dick Sheppard's romantic vision in 1914 that shaped St Martin-in-the-Fields throughout the twentieth century as the 'church of the ever-open door':

> I saw a great church standing in the greatest Square in the greatest City in the world . . . There passed me into its warm inside hundreds and hundreds of all sorts of people, going up to the temple of their Lord, with all their difficulties, trials and sorrows . . . I saw it full of people, dropping in at all hours of the day and night. It was never dark, it was lighted all night and all day, and often tired bits of humanity swept in. And I said to them as they passed: 'Where are you going?' And they said only one thing, 'This is our home. This is where we are going to learn of the love of Jesus Christ. This is the Altar of our Lord where all our peace lies. This is St Martin's.'[3]

Third, a parish church is a room with a view committed to looking beyond itself to God, and to the kingdom of God as seen in the life, death and resurrection of Jesus Christ. This metaphor alludes to the image of God's home in John 14. Jesus said to the disciples, 'In my Father's house there are many dwelling places [or rooms]. If it were not so would I have told you that I go to prepare a place for you?'

God's dwelling place is capacious. All sorts of people find their home there, people as diverse as Matthew the tax-collector, doubting Thomas, and impulsive and unreliable Peter. It would be a lot easier to create communities of the likeminded, but if parish churches are going to point beyond themselves to the sort of community that God is collecting, then we had better take the trouble to ensure that parish churches are broad, inclusive communities.

So *A Room with a View* is intended to suggest that the English parish church is, or should aspire to be, a broad Christian community, open particularly to the poor, and alive to the glory of God who was in Christ reconciling the world.

The present context

It is now commonplace to admit that we in Britain have a problem that is both personal and institutional about the credibility of Christian belief. For longer than our lifetimes our churches have suffered numeric decline and reducing influence. What was described as 'secularization' now looks different and more complex. Religion is as much a part of human self-understanding and expression as ever. In the last British census, 42 million identified themselves as 'Christian'. What this means is less than clear.

At a local, parochial level, in 1941 there were 1,568 on the Electoral Roll of St Martin's. In 2008 the number was 311. The pressure to survive can distort our purpose. In this context Jesus' saying about our being willing to lose our life for the sake of the kingdom of heaven is heard less as promise and more as judgement. I was struck a few years ago to hear a bishop say that he was not prepared to be a bishop of a dying church. Perhaps we can guess what he meant, but in saying this, the pressure to be successful had caused him to step away from the pattern of Jesus Christ and put too much store in a particular institutional form of Christianity.

The Church of England, relieved to find anything that helps stem the decline in numbers, has got fixated on a narrow range of evangelistic basic Christian education programmes and on what are called 'fresh expressions of being church'. There is energy here, and for that we can be grateful, but this renewal movement tends to be self-consciously church centred. Research by Bob Jackson shows that London Diocesan clergy take on average fewer baptisms, weddings and funerals than clergy in any other diocese:

> Far from being a problem to them, the lack of occasional offices . . . has enabled them to focus on building the gathered community . . . It seems fairly well accepted in London Diocese that a pastoral ministry and way into the local community . . . is not the way forward. It is certainly true that London clergy are performing on average very few occasional offices. Yet church attendance is rising.[4]

In a stringent critique of the widely influential report *A Mission-Shaped Church*, Professor John Hull concluded that what was being offered was a church-shaped mission[5] that does less than justice to the mission of God who 'so loved *the world* that he gave his only Son' (John 3.16).

Parochial clergy, particularly those with historic buildings, sometimes complain that they are not 'museum keepers', but there could be worse things for a priest to be. My experience of living in Trafalgar Square has made me realize that London's museums and galleries have been enjoying an enviable renaissance. It is striking how they seek to engage people's interests in a variety of ways with a lively appeal to different personality types, and people with varied interests, abilities and time availability. This has set me thinking about the different ways in which people relate to a parish church – St Martin-in-the-Fields.

Of course what we are primarily is a 'eucharistic community', but there is more than one way of belonging to a church. It ought to be obvious that people at different stages of faith or commitment, of different personality types and interests, and at different stages of their life, will be drawn by and capable of different things in relation to church. This is certainly modelled in the Church of England's contemporary pluralism, but every parish church has to recognize and provide for it.

So I want to sketch seven ways in which people legitimately relate to the sort of parish church that is 'a room with a view'. Inevitably this draws heavily on my experience at St Martin-in-the-Fields, and of course I recognize the particularities of that church. However, the same points could be made from any of the parishes in which I have ministered – in Stepney, Lincoln and on the Isle of Dogs. Whilst there are tensions and problems facing the Church of England at a local level – there always will be – my aim is to encourage and develop a sustainable model of ministry that is committed to the parish that is the world, and not just the congregation.

The eucharistic community

Churches are primarily about worship. Being a baptized member of the eucharistic community is the most obvious way of being part of any parish church. It is the core group doing the core task without which nothing else has any place. The Eucharist has it all. Its different names emphasize different aspects of its work. Holy Communion, Eucharist, Mass, emphasize our community with each other growing out of our communion with God; that we gather primarily to give thanks and praise to God; and at the end we are sent out, dismissed, to the mission of God.

We have also recognized that, like many London churches, St Martin's is an international church. Like every church I have ever known, only more so, St Martin's has active international partnerships with church and development agencies in Hong Kong and China, India, South Africa, Malawi, Kenya, Uganda and the West Indies. Our visitors from around the world add greatly to this.

Jesus said, 'Where two or three are gathered in my name I am there among them' (Matthew 18.20). So the community is essential to a Christianity that is not just about private, personal experience. The trouble is that, as a rabbi once said, 'Where there are three Jews, you will have four opinions.' That is true of any group, and usually disagreements are resolved in favour of the most powerful, but it is part of the purpose of the eucharistic community to model diversity, confident in the unity of God and of the eucharistic action given us by Christ.

One of the most enjoyable liturgical developments over recent years at St Martin's has been our giving much greater emphasis to the celebration of Pentecost. Through it we have come to an enriched theology of the Holy Spirit, the breath or wind of God, the energizing fire that burns with both zeal and judgement. The big gift of the Holy Spirit at Pentecost is communication. People who did not speak the same language found that they understood each other. That is what happens when people meet in the spirit of love.

So at Pentecost we have a single Eucharist for the Chinese- and English-speaking congregations. The 'Chinese congregations' means two languages, Cantonese and Mandarin. In the 'English-speaking congregations' a significant number of people have different first languages. This is relatively easy territory in a London church now. We enjoy the ethnic and cultural mix, people's ability to speak several languages, perform different sorts of music and provide wonderfully varied food for lunch. It is a terrific window into our being a worldwide church.

The eucharistic community is not static: it is a dynamic and changing group. Always there are issues that put our diversity to the test. Most days I pray in front of an icon of Li Tim Oi, the first Anglican woman priest. This has been helpful because one of the least satisfactory parts of the *Windsor Report* of the Lambeth Commission on communion[6] was its use of the ordination of women as a model of change within the communion. They start with the ordination of Li Tim Oi in a pastoral emergency in Macau in 1944 but say nothing of what went before. Change has a history. Dick Sheppard was campaigning for the ordination of women in the run-up to the 1930 Lambeth Conference. The publication of his *The Impatience of a Parson*[7] strained his friendship with Archbishop Lang, and Sheppard was widely thought by the church hierarchy to be irresponsible.

In 1942 Reinhold Niebuhr had said to Bishop R. O. Hall, the Bishop of Hong Kong, that it would make a tremendous difference if a woman were actually ordained. Before Li Tim Oi's ordination Hall consulted the Archbishop of Canterbury. Archbishop Temple's reply arrived after Li Tim Oi's ordination on 24 January 1944. Interestingly in the present context, he wrote that this seems to be primarily a matter for one's own Province. However, he went on to counsel for a revocable temporary expedient in the exceptional circumstances.[8]

The Windsor Report's main concern was with unity, not with change. In considering the ordination of women it jumped from 1944 to the Lambeth Conference of 1968, but this was not change led by the hierarchy and councils of the church. The ordinations of Jane Hwang and Joyce Bennett in Hong Kong in 1971 and of the first women priests in other Provinces were actions in a turbulent process of 'reception' of women priests by the Anglican communion. Change is often disruptive. At the outset, change is not always consensual. Nor is it necessarily led by the hierarchy.

In September 2003, after Jeffrey John did not become Bishop of Reading, the PCC of St Martin's voted unanimously to sign up to both Inclusive Church, of which I have become a Trustee, and Changing Attitudes. It seemed a relatively easy decision and was communicated to the congregations. What little comment this received was positive. St Martin's is an open and tolerant community and has a fairly visible gay minority in the congregation. Two months later, some people were beginning to express their discomfort. A group of West Africans, one of whom said she had thought about leaving St Martin's, and some of the Chinese congregation, raised their concerns. Interestingly, a South Indian was more concerned about Gene Robinson's having been divorced than his being gay. At the Annual Meeting the following April the matter came up again, as if for the first time, some people feeling that their views had been taken for granted.

As is often the case with moral issues, even when the Bible is clear – as with divorce and remarriage, pacifism, or the swearing of oaths – there are genuine differences between Christians. Whenever our members have raised the positive acceptance of homosexuals as a problem, there has been a conversation. A high point in this process was when a senior Nigerian layman, a member of his own Diocesan Synod, who had come to our daily services for about six months, asked to meet me. We discussed homosexuality because what we were saying was different from what the church at home was teaching. At the end of our hour he still disagreed with me and concluded, 'But this is not an issue to divide us.' Although I am aware of some of the gay members of the church drifting away over the last few years, I am not aware of anyone leaving St Martin's over our having taken a positively inclusive stand.

In a lecture on 'The Future of the Anglican Communion', Bishop David Beetge, a member of the Lambeth Commission that produced *The Windsor Report*, said, 'We are not in Communion because we agree or are likeminded but because Jesus said, "Do this in remembrance of me".'[9]

Every parish church is an international, diverse eucharistic community open to change led by the Holy Spirit. Each eucharistic community makes a particular contribution to the Anglican communion by being 'the world's local church'.

Other ways of belonging to church

In 2003 there was a very interesting congregational consultation at St Martin's about the reordering of our buildings. We were considering creating a baptistry in the central porch, or placing the font on the central axis of the main entrance, to show that it is the point of entry into the community of faith. Significant disquiet was expressed from the members of our eucharistic community because so many people did not arrive that way but came to St Martin's not fitting the norms, unconventionally. Baptism might be what celebrates and seals people having made their way in by other means.

So the eucharistic community is the core, but is only one way of describing a parish church which is much richer, more interesting and diverse than can be summarized by numbers on the membership list, or as those who are baptized and receiving Communion.

A community of service

In John's account of the Last Supper we are given an action to demonstrate the new commandment to love one another as Christ has loved us. Washing feet is as distinctive an act for the Christian community as breaking bread. St Martin-in-the-

Fields has an unusual reputation for Christian service and charity understood as 'love in action'. It stems from the life of our patron saint, St Martin of Tours, who shared his cloak with a beggar who returned to him as Christ. 'For as much as you did it to one of the least of these, you did it to me' (Matthew 25.40).

Yet most parish churches have an extensive and honourable list of charitable groups meeting in and around the church. Served by committed people who are not necessarily part of the eucharistic community, they act in loving service. On the Isle of Dogs, for example, there were Alcoholics Anonymous, a toy library, an open youth club, the Docklands Drugs Initiative and local Relief in Need and children's charities. These sorts of groups are enabled by a hospitable eucharistic community and they also help to inform and educate that community.

Charity is one aspect of foot-washing, the search for justice another. In the 1980s the Archbishop's Commission on Urban Priority Areas recognized that it was not enough to state moral principles but to go on to identify the political implications of those principles. On the Isle of Dogs this approach was put to the test in 1993 when Britain's first (openly racist) British National Party councillor was elected in a by-election. In the absence of political leadership from the local Labour and Liberal Democrat parties, who imploded under accusations of racism, the local churches took a lead. For nine months we worked to create broad community alliances to address the underlying issues: housing, telling the truth about race, building bridges with the local Bengali community, as well as strengthening the local democratic political parties and increasing the electoral turnout at the main election. The then Bishop of Stepney, Richard Chartres, commented, 'It's difficult not to be political when Jesus said, "Love your neighbour" and one political party is engaged in a sustained campaign of hatred against one particular group of neighbours.'[10]

A vision of social justice brings with it a commitment to change the world. In 2005 an all-night event called 'Wake Up for Trade Justice' attracted 25,000 people to Whitehall. Many were from churches, but it seemed wider, inclusive of anyone who wanted to identify with this campaign. 'Everyone who loves is born of God and knows God' (1 John 4.7), whether they know it or not. The commitment of these people to justice can challenge the eucharistic community.

It is easy to see why for St John an act of loving service is central to the remembrance of Christ. Church as a community of service is another way of people identifying with this Christian community.

A place of prayer

If there was one thing that caught me by surprise after my ordination as Deacon, it was the instant and immediate importance of intercessory prayer. At the early services in St Dunstan's, Stepney, in that first week of ordained ministry in October 1979, I was completely caught up in praying for people and things, holding them and their life's events before God – not just the congregation but the parish. It is one of many things for which I am indebted to my training incumbent, Father Norry McCurry. Intercessory prayer has been an important part of my role as a priest ever since. It is, of course, what people expect. For ten years nearly every Sunday one of the market traders who used to be outside St Martin's said, 'Say one for me'. It is what a priest is for.

When we open the church each morning at about 7.45 a.m., one of the first people through the door is a woman on her way to work. She kneels for about two minutes and leaves. It is what church is for, a place of prayer. Just inside the door of St Martin's is a Prayer Board on which people pin their own prayers or requests for prayers. Serious business is done there:

In Memory of Mrs Woosnam – buried today.

Please pray for my baby who was lost to me one month ago before it could be baptized.

Help me to get a job and a home.

Peace.

And the delightfully ambiguous:

Please pray for my beloved fiancé – may his eyes heal quickly.

Some of them reminded me of T. S. Eliot's lines in 'Ash-Wednesday' about the veiled sister praying for the children at the gate who would not go away and could not pray.

It is the widely recognized calling and purpose of clergy and churches to pray for others, for people in need, for the world. It is also a core task to teach people to pray and to provide spaces in which it is easy to pray.

Back in my earliest days of ordained ministry I used to do an occasional half-day chaplaincy in St Paul's Cathedral. On one of these occasions I was exhausted and chose for 15 minutes every hour to kneel down in the transept and pray. Each time I knelt down I was the only person doing so. Each time I got up, there were four, ten and seven other people kneeling nearby. It was as if the purpose of the building needed to be demonstrated for others to join in.

Christian formation involves active participation in a community of prayer: prayer groups, an occasional course to 'teach us to pray', a weekend retreat. In Lincoln in the mid-1980s we organized an individually guided retreat through Lent for 57 people. It still impacts on some of our lives. At St Martin's lay people lead the saying of weekday Evening Prayer and the intercessions at the Sunday 10 a.m. Eucharist. Douglas Board's recent book *The Naked Year* has emerged partly from his leading of our Sunday intercessions. His prayers engage the realities of our world and our own lives before God.[11]

When people come in to a church, what matters most is that it is a 'thin' place between heaven and earth; in another of Eliot's phrases, 'where prayer has been valid' ('Little Gidding'). Such churches are spacious, hospitable and inspiring. The late Peter Benenson told me that the idea of Amnesty International came to him in St Martin-in-the-Fields. 'You would say it was prayer. All I can say is that the idea came from outside of me'. To which my response could only be, 'Thanks be to God'.

Learning and the God of truth

Christians have always been concerned with education for its own sake because we believe that God is of truth. There is a practical depth to the church's involvement in education, ranging from higher education to parish Sunday Schools.

There is a crossover from the church's public provision of education into Christian formation and faith education. Some churches and clergy may feel under pressure from those who come to church to qualify for church school admissions, but the Church of England is justly proud of its schools. Clearly these are another way in which people belong to the local church.

Despite this, it is commonly agreed that large numbers of people now lack what the Bishop of London calls 'a Christian grammar'. A recent description of the process of secularization has emphasized our failure to transmit the Christ story down the generations.[12] Faith education is therefore of paramount importance to the Church. The Diocese of London has a policy that every parish should run a Christian basics course like Alpha or Emmaus. For many churches these have been points of numerical growth. They have also given lay people an increased confidence in what is partly a knowledge-based organization. However, such courses do not appeal to everyone and part of the price of such widespread commitment to 'Christian basics' is a perceived 'dumbing down' of the Church's educational offer.

For some years we have been looking to develop a Christian basics course that might fit St Martin's and have come to the conclusion that the people who come to us are not looking for a structured A to Z of Christian faith that systematically explores key themes of Christian theology. Instead, the St Martin's community draws people because we begin our theological reflection in the context of global events, human relationships, social change, and a commitment to engage with the reality of life as lived by all of us. So we develop a theological conversation through liturgies, sermons, 'thought pieces' and educational events. Some of these are re-presented in small publications that have proved very popular, with titles such as, *Life after Life: An Exploration of Living, Dying and Whatever Comes Next*; *Voices of Harvest*; *Christianity and Homosexuality*; and *In Search of Healing*. The contributors are clergy and laity, from within the St Martin's community and beyond, something that resonates with our intention to produce a resource in conversation with each other.

Education courses are also part of the public offer that draws in people who are not otherwise members but who are interested in the subject. For example, two years ago a Lent series of talks called 'Beyond Church' attracted attendance of between 60 and 100 people, many of whom had no evident link with St Martin's but who were interested in a well-informed discussion of difficult moral issues. A public meeting in advance of the war in Iraq drew 160 people. When we have worked with the National Gallery's education programme we have drawn similarly large numbers, only some of whom are from our own congregations.

An education programme is one more way in which people

who are not necessarily part of the eucharistic community might feel they belong to their church in what is a serious search for the God of truth.

Creativity and the arts

On Good Friday St Martin's has a well-attended three hours' service from 12 noon to 3 p.m. Something like 450 people come to all or part of it. It is preceded by a short 'all age' service at 10 a.m. attended by 70 or 80. In the evening there is a concert. Whether it's one of the Bach Passions or the Mozart *Requiem*, all 825 seats are always sold out. Concerts attract audiences that are different from those which attend services. This is part of the change that has happened to institutional Christianity in this country. It is bad for church attendance figures, but it is not all loss. There are deep Christian cultural roots in our society.

There is an astonishingly accomplished musical life to St Martin's, but it is only different in scale from what happens in many parish churches. I grew up singing in a parish church choir where the organist and choirmaster also ran the local choral society. On the Isle of Dogs we had occasional concerts and in 1992 the London Docklands Singers were formed by one of the congregation attracting singers from the local community and they have sung in a performance of *The Dream of Gerontius* in St Paul's Cathedral.

With at least six concerts every week, St Martin's is one of London's major concert venues. I don't know that there is any strong association with the worshipping life of the church, but I do know that to sit in church listening to wonderful music is one way of being recreated in the heart of the city. It can be healing and Godly.

Some of our best work with homeless people and young people at risk has been in this area of creative arts. Exhibiting paintings, or playing music and receiving applause, is terrific for self-esteem – quite apart from the fun of making something beautiful. When this has been taken into an act of worship in church, the contributions have been made with striking reverence by people who are not habitually at public worship.

In the twentieth century St Martin's was best known for its ethics, but there is an earlier tradition of aesthetics, offering to God the best of art and beauty. You can see it in the architecture. St Martin's is one of London's most beautiful eighteenth-century churches, the work of James Gibbs and some of the most accomplished craftsmen of the 1720s. The planned renewal of the buildings is an opportunity to commission new works of art of similar quality. The new Christmas crib by Tomoaki Suzuki for Trafalgar Square was the first of a small number of high quality and important commissions. It has been followed by a new east window in the church by Shirazeh Houshiary and Pip Horne, and a poem by Andrew Motion for a handrail around the light-well in Church Path, connecting the inner and outer realities for the passer-by. The willingness of the artistic community to be involved has been humbling. The creativity of God means that parish churches can be marvellous centres of artistic creativity, and this, too, provides a way for many people to make an offering to God.

Honest commercial exchange

St Martin's is known throughout the world for music and feeding people. Given our location, it is not so surprising that we have also been able to sell these goods to people who can afford to pay for them, extending our ministry commercially. Our concerts make a profit and receive no funding from the Arts Council. The Café in the Crypt has been London's *Les Routiers* Café of the Year. St Martin's is London's twentieth most visited tourist attraction.

This experiment in business was set up in the 1980s by my

predecessor, Canon Geoffrey Brown. In some ways it offered a commercial alternative to the sorts of urban and social regeneration proposed by the Archbishop's Commission on Urban Priority Areas who produced the report *Faith in the City*.[13] At that time, providing employment was a key aim for St Martin's, but so was providing an income to stabilize ailing church finances.

Making an honest profit was seen to be good, and a number of senior business people have given their time to oversee this project at Board level. One said how refreshing it was to be part of a Christian church that appreciated his working life and skills as a blessing. Given the amount of time many of us spend at work, that still seems to me a serious indictment of what most parish churches pray for and get concerned about. Having a business at St Martin's has created employment and has indeed been good for the church's finances. As with our social work at The Connection at St Martin's, we do not require staff to be communicant Christians but ask that they share and put into practice our common values.

The business has also provided different ways for visitors to engage with the church. It used to be said that the task of the most visited churches was to turn tourists into pilgrims. Customers keep more control than that. A customer pays for something he or she wants – food, music, a brass rubbing or whatever. This is not about customers becoming part of the eucharistic community, though sometimes they do. It is about customers being satisfied by a good and honest commercial encounter with a Christian church that establishes an honest and trustworthy relationship. This is important because a recent survey found that only 43 per cent said they trust the Church. This is fewer than trust the educational service and about half the rating for the armed forces.[14] Trust and credibility have to be earned.

The increased number of visitors has also added energy to the place. It is a pleasure to come into such a thriving and vibrant church. The professionalism of the business means we look after our buildings better than we did and provide better for the casual visitor. The Parochial Church Council is also more businesslike and has a three-year Mission Action Plan. Having a Chief Executive running St Martin-in-the-Fields Ltd alongside me as Vicar has proved to be a very creative dynamic. It is interesting to see the commercial model of Church being imitated.

A place for the whole community

Parish churches are important focal points in local communities. They are one of the few public places where people gather. As places of memory they also collect a community's history. This is an incredibly important function and a strong reason for all the members of the local community to support their parish church.

The significance of this is well made by Simon Jenkins. His Introduction to *England's Thousand Best Churches* refers to our parish churches as the 'museums of England'. He respects the church as 'a shrine of impenetrable mystery'. Into these churches people have poured their faith, joy, sorrow, labour, love. Jenkins says, 'The local parish church is like Thomas Gray's tombstone. It tells of "homely joys and destiny obscure . . . the short and simple annals of the poor"'.[15]

Simon Jenkins dwells on the physical fabric of the church that embodies this historic role, but it is a continuing contemporary experience through the Church's occasional offices for parishioners who have not necessarily been part of the congregation – weddings, funerals, and, at St Martins, memorial services. To work well, these have to be honest and 'real'. That often means they have to be 'personalized'. I am struck that I have rarely felt compromised by this.

That holy places are for the whole community is the reason why admission charges to cathedrals and churches are a disaster. They subvert the relationship by creating tourists, not pilgrims. If finance is a problem, and it is, admissions charges are the wrong answer. It would be better to keep the main body of the great centres of Christianity open and accessible to all, while charging to go in to areas of special interest and strengthening the commercial side through associated activities, as is the case with the café and concerts at St Martin's.

Nearly always, people are respectful of Church even if they are not themselves active members. What the minister often meets in these settings is people who know about love, justice, mercy, joy, celebration, loss and grief in ways that suggest they are not far from the kingdom of heaven even though they themselves would mostly not name it as such.

By fulfilling the core commitments of a church, the eucharistic community makes it possible for the holy place to be accessible to others. It opens the church as a place of honest encounter for the world before God.

Conclusion

Today's Church of England lives with the pressures of institutional survival. It cannot be guaranteed. Under this pressure we also live in a time of great energy and creativity. What I have described is, at its best, not just adaptability but faithfulness to God. It is not a faith in the immortality of our own institutions. The heart of the gospel is in the paradox of our being willing to lose our lives to find them.

When people complain that the Church of England washes its dirty linen in public it is tempting to reply with Eliot again that at least we are washing it. Beyond the local parish we are not sure how we belong together, but to belong everywhere you have to belong somewhere. So I am convinced that the problems of the Anglican communion will be answered best in the local parish church. I have tried to describe the experience of a parish church that is open to the world, to the poor and to the vision of God's many-roomed generosity. In its local form, it is a worldwide diverse church. Led by the Spirit of God, it is open to change in every generation. Of course there is a gap between aspiration and reality, but we have been given a vision of God's kingdom and that gap is something Christians have always had to handle.

Perhaps the key to the churches in which I have been privileged to minister is the way in which they welcome people. Every church says it is welcoming but the test is whether the visitors bring anything that is valued, wanted, will change the life of the parish church and not just be assimilated into it so that the only people who belong are the people who fit the existing community. The test is whether we really do expect to meet Christ in the stranger.

'A room with a view' is a way of being an open church that requires a generosity of spirit and trust in God. In the crucial dynamic between kingdom, church and world, it assumes that God is at work in the world, where the kingdom of God will come as it is in heaven, and that the parish church's task is to witness to this in many and various ways.

CHAPTER 2

The poor are always with you: a sideways view

When I announced we would be leaving the Isle of Dogs at the heart of east London's Docklands and moving to St Martin-in-the-Fields there were three quite distinct reactions from the church congregation. The professional incomers said, 'That's a good move', with an unspoken surprise that wondered, 'How did you get that?' People from the Commonwealth, their eyes misty with tears, said, 'That is the church we knew before we came to London' (because of St Martin's broadcasting on the BBC World Service). But the reaction of nearly all the east-enders was, 'Where? Where did you say you are going?'

For many people, especially poorer people, London does not function as a single city. People stick to their patch, where they are comfortable. Many people on the Isle of Dogs at that time didn't even go into the new developments because they weren't for them. But neither did they perceive the centre of London as theirs – something Ken Livingstone as the first Mayor of London has tried to address by using Trafalgar Square for cultural events.

In 1995 some of the congregation on the Isle of Dogs thought that by leaving the east end for the West End I was going up-market and leaving them behind. In a sense they were right. The conspicuous wealth of the West End is evident. St Martin's is known as the 'Royal Parish Church' and Downing Street and the government offices in Whitehall are in the parish. But the truth is that I moved up- and down-market in one move. St Martin's is also the church of many who are homeless and who come to the centre of London to get lost or to be found. The Connection at St Martin's cares for them, young people at risk as well as older people who are homeless or at risk of homelessness.

St Martin-in-the-Fields, in a way that typifies the best of English parish churches, is a big, broad, inclusive and open community. It is a model community in which we find ourselves in relation to our neighbours, including the poorest in our city.

A sideways view

Most of us look at poverty sideways. As a parish priest, I am not poor but I have sat alongside poor people in a variety of contexts. Sitting beside, I have a sideways view at poverty. Have you noticed that people rarely look directly at a street beggar? We tend to be uncertain or embarrassed and look out of the corner of our eye. We are unsettled by poverty, or by the challenge of a beggar, or by our inability to know what adequately to do. That's a sideways view of poverty as well.

To this the Christian gospel is a daily challenge, and the story of St Martin himself exemplifies it. Martin was a Roman soldier in the fourth century. On a cold winter's day, when riding out of the gate of Amiens in northern France, Martin saw a beggar cold and naked. He cut his cloak in two and gave half to the beggar. That night in a dream the beggar returned to him as Christ, an echo of Jesus in Matthew's Gospel: 'For as much as you did it to one of the least of these you did it to me.'

So the Christian has an expectation of meeting Christ particularly in the poor, the marginal and the outcast, and of receiving strangers as if they were Christ. Only sometimes has this been my experience. The daily round of difficult people is pretty grinding. One of my predecessors, Austen Williams, who had a reputation as a pastor and a listener, told a story against himself. He was rushing between the vicarage and church when a man accosted him. 'Remember me?' said the man. Austen, late and in a hurry, asked, 'How much do you want?' 'I only wanted to know that you remember me,' the man replied, evidently crushed.

There is a Christian duty to listen to poor people especially because the kingdom of God is said by Jesus to be very near in them, perhaps because they have least to lose in changing the *status quo* of our society. This is not easy either, because poor people are curiously invisible. Engage them and they can be difficult as they often see things on a slant, are not easy to hear or interpret, and can be as unreasonable, or more so, as anyone else. Yet they also often see things clearly in a way that some others who have more to lose do not.

The work with homeless people typically begins with the very basic provisions: feeding, washing, clothing, and providing a place of safety and warmth. In this context it is possible to build relationships of trust and gain confidence. Homelessness is never a single issue. The people who come to us have been affected by the breakdown of relationships, unemployment, mental illness, addictions and debilitating poverty, as well as by not having a home. It can be a slow process, for many of the people we see have been badly damaged. A few years ago, a young man slept on the south side of the church and came to Morning Prayer every day for months. When he eventually spoke he said, very slowly, 'If you haven't spoken for a long time, you can't find the words.'

The task is not just to sustain people in these circumstances, though that is important, but to help people gain self-confidence, a sense of their own worth and of having some control over their circumstances. The life-changing work happens one to one or in groups. We have a resettlement group where people learn to shop, budget and cook, the sort of life skills most of us take for granted. There are groups for people with particular needs such as alcohol or drug addictions. But surprisingly it's the education programme, sport (particularly for the youngsters), and the music, art and creative writing groups where extraordinary things happen.

The dimensions of poverty

There is an interesting difference between the Beatitudes in the Gospels of Luke and Matthew. In Matthew, Jesus speaks his Sermon on the Mount, whereas in Luke it is given on the level, the Sermon on the Plain. In Matthew, Jesus says, 'Blessed are the poor in spirit, for theirs is the kingdom of heaven' (Matthew 5.3), but in Luke he says much more directly, 'Blessed are *you* who are poor, for yours is the kingdom of God' (Luke 6.20).

There is considerable interest at the moment in redefining the way we understand our wealth and also, therefore, our poverty. We are used to thinking of this in economic terms, but it also includes our psychological, social and spiritual sense of well-being. It is striking how evenings in the West End of London begin with such energy and promise, happy people meeting in the early evening for a good night out. In St Martin's Place this tips over at about 11.30 p.m. when for some people the evening has gone wrong and they have fallen out, often having drunk too much. To the onlooker, binge drinking does not look uplifting. City bonuses or a big win on the Lottery do not buy happiness, though many of us might like the chance to find that out for ourselves. The widening gap between richest and poorest in our country is one of the factors associated with social discontent.

The Greater London Authority's Cultural Strategy struck me as poor in spirit. How could a cultural strategy be a spirituality-free zone in which the discussion of values is pathetically restricted to 'value for money'? We, not just the GLA, have so lost confidence in religious belief and language that we do not know how to discriminate between good religion and bad. At best we accept a broad and uncritical tolerance – there are many paths up the mountain, so if that's what you believe and it doesn't harm anyone else, that's fine by me. At worst we descend into ignorant bigotry to defend our own religious tribe. In a world where religion frequently demonstrates its capacity to be lethal, we would do well to rediscover an ability to be critical and discerning in matters of the spirit. Matthew's 'poor in spirit' can seem pretty widespread in London today, and not in ways that seem a blessing.

In one modern translation of the Bible, this Beatitude reads, 'How blessed are those who know their need of God.' That's much more like it to my mind. Without God there is a poverty of spirit. The blessing is not in the emptiness but in the *realization* of our emptiness, knowing our need of God. This is much too important a task to be left to our churches, synagogues, temples and mosques, and it is a good thing that public bodies have begun to recognize its significance.

In Luke's Gospel the first blessing of the Sermon on the Plain is directed to material poverty. It is difficult to know whether the best descriptions of poverty are statistics or stories. How do we define who is poor? In the 1980s one of the congregation on the Isle of Dogs was affronted by the report of the Archbishop of Canterbury's Commission on Urban Priority Areas (*Faith in the City*). It listed some of the indicators of poverty and included having an outside toilet. She said, 'Who says? My husband always thought it was unhealthy when they put the toilet inside the house.' So there is an element of subjectivity here.

Government works on an objective definition of poverty when households have less than 60 per cent of the national average disposable income. Why 60 per cent is a matter of subjective or political judgement about the level below which people lack the resources to obtain the types of diet, participate in the activities and live in conditions that are widely thought to be necessary in our society.

Our national assumptions are that there is much less poverty in prosperous London than, say, in Wales, Northern Ireland and the north east of England. But the Greater London Authority has identified that if housing costs and child care are added to our fixed outgoings the proportion of households in inner London with less than 60 per cent of the average disposable income is an astonishing 53 per cent, far higher than for any of the regions. In 2007 a report for Barclays Bank showed that in Kensington and Chelsea the average annual household income was £101,600, by far the highest in the country. In Tower Hamlets, my old borough and not quite the poorest in London, 12 per cent of households have a gross annual income of £10,000 or less. Poverty affects everything: health and morbidity as well as educational achievement and the general sense of well-being.

If that is not your experience and you want to know what that feels like, Polly Toynbee's *Hard Work: Life in Low-Pay Britain*[1] is a useful book to read. She and a number of other well-known figures were challenged by Church Action on Poverty to live just for the six weeks of Lent in 2002 on what was then the minimum wage of £4.10 an hour. Her experience of how things cost much more when you lack the financial ability to exercise choice, and of quickly getting into debt, is salutary. Or look at the adverts in the *Sun* or *Mirror*. They often have more than a page of lenders offering unsecured loans at ridiculously high interest rates.

That the eradication of child poverty is one of the government's stated objectives is very much to its credit, but it is an extremely difficult target to achieve. In a residential community in east London, on estates adjacent to the Isle of Dogs Enterprise Zone, there were households with three generations unemployed, and people whose isolation was compounded by their poverty. In 2004 there was a controversial advertising campaign by the children's charity, Barnardo's. The first picture showed a newborn baby with a cockroach crawling out of his mouth. Another featured a baby with a methylated spirits bottle in its mouth. A third showed a baby with a syringe. The headline said: 'There are no silver spoons for children born into poverty'. But if poor people in general are invisible in the places of power and wealth, as tends to be the case, this sort of publicity is a good thing. The campaign was designed to emphasize two things. First, the extent of child poverty in Britain today: Barnardo's claimed that 3.9 million children live in poverty, a higher figure than for any other country in the European Union. Second, it emphasized that poverty is repeated from generation to generation and is difficult to escape from.

Mind the gap

Because the definition of poverty is relative, the poor will always be with us, as Jesus said. Yet as a society we are obsessed with the other end of the scale. Each year the *Sunday Times* publishes a 'Rich List'. I once saw a vagrant in St Martin's Place lying in front of an *Evening Standard* billboard proclaiming: 'Chris Evans £7 million payout'. There is a proper and growing concern about the gap between the richest and poorest. The obscene stories of rich footballers frittering their money away sometimes defies belief, as with the East European footballer who allegedly boasted of standing in front of a beggar burning money to emphasize the gap between them.

On the Isle of Dogs in the early 1990s, some of the new private estates not only retained sections of the old dock walls to divide them from the neighbouring council estates, they also added barbed wire to the top to make sure that people couldn't climb across. A black South African friend said it looked like 'economic apartheid'.

A great thing about the Docklands development was the energy and inward investment it brought. Some people in the business community really wanted to help make improvements for the local residential community. The London Docklands Development Corporation (LDDC) itself sponsored a number of initiatives to improve local schools. Sometimes the gap in experience was very telling, as when the primary school at which I was Chair of Governors received a gift of computers in the late 1980s, one for each classroom. The computers were delivered before the LDDC realized they would also have to pay for a second electrical socket to be provided in each classroom if the gift was going to be useful.

There is a great deal of concern about 'City fat cats' who are paid salaries and bonuses out of all proportion to the rest of us. One of the difficulties with Docklands is the juxtaposition of conspicuous wealth alongside (mostly in parallel with and therefore looking sideways at and not connecting with) some of the poorest in Britain.

On 19 October 2003 the *Observer* carried a fascinating article by Nick Cohen headlined 'A tale of two cities'. It described that year's HSBC Annual General Meeting in which The East London Community Organisation (TELCO) confronted the bank's chairman, Sir John Bond, with a demand for a living wage for the bank's cleaners. Apparently the cleaners are paid £5 an hour and TELCO were pressing for £6.50. Abdul Durrant, the cleaner who made the case for TELCO, was said to supplement his wages with a second cleaning job and by minicabbing at weekends. It is easy to feel the force of his case.

Sir John Bond responded by emphasizing the importance of the principle of the market rate for the job. In other words, even a firm as big as HSBC operates within a market and is not free to do whatever it wants. It has to survive against the competition. Sir John emphasized HSBC's outstanding record of charitable giving, at which point the Roman Catholic Bishop of Brentwood shouted out, 'We don't want your charity, we want justice.' The Bishop's moral force was overwhelming and he won the day because the major banks on Canary Wharf now pay their cleaners a living wage – but the Chairman of the bank also had a point, which didn't work in this case because the sums involved were insignificant in comparison to HSBC's profits.

There is much to be said in favour of socially responsible capitalism. If HSBC fails, they will not be able to pay salaries, let alone make charitable donations. As a student I was struck by a letter from Karl Marx written in the early 1870s to J. M. Ludlow, the parliamentary draftsman of much of the legislation that enabled the co-operative movement in the 1850s. In it Marx said that the process of liberal change in England was such that there would not be a revolution here as had happened elsewhere in Europe. This is a very English model of change.

London has some significant examples of socially responsible capitalism – like London First, Business in the Community and the Prince's Trust. St Martin-in-the-Fields has needed this in the £36 million renewal of its buildings. The work was much needed, long overdue and will equip St Martin's to serve London through the twenty-first century. The Heritage Lottery Fund gave £15 million and the rest had to be raised from companies, trusts and public sources, with the largest contributions coming from wealthy individuals.

What is said about wealth in the New Testament is more varied than the radical passages in the Gospels about giving away all your possessions. At the end of the First Letter to Timothy there are fascinating instructions for the wealthy to use their riches well rather than give everything away:

> As for those who in the present age are rich, command them not to be haughty, or to set their hopes on the uncertainty of riches, but rather on God who richly provides us with everything for our enjoyment. They are to do good, to be rich in good works, generous and ready to share, thus storing up for themselves the treasure of a good foundation for the future, so that they may take hold of the life that really is life. (1 Timothy 6.17–19)

One aspect of the St Martin's buildings renewal project is to create excellent facilities for the poorest of the poor in the heart of London. It's not the cheapest place to do so, but poor people gravitate to the centre of the capital. The poor will always be with us, and it is better for London as a whole if we plan to include them, as they cannot be designed out.

We could not have got this project to birth if our neighbours, especially our business neighbours, had not given us a very great deal of charitable help. None has tried to impose conditions on their giving, and I assume donors expect us to continue not just to care for the poor but also to give voice to the poor. There is something very healthy about a society that supports, pays for and engages in the necessary conflicts that are involved in the process of liberal change.

Values and vision

I visited an old lady in hospital at the end of her life. For several days, if the doctors or nurses were busy doing something for her, I would be asked to wait until they had finished. Then the day came when the doctor made way for me. I knew that Violet would die that day. It is for this reason that I am anxious when government rediscovers the importance of religion for the building of community. Politicians and others tend to make way for religion when they themselves have nothing left to offer. Whilst the churches are pleased that government has recently acknowledged the significance of faith communities, we should also be concerned about what that implies about the breakdown of community. We might also be less than sure about our ability as churches to turn things round.

In Docklands, the London Docklands Development Corporation made community development a priority only after they had been in existence more than five years and had done a great deal to destroy the local community that had been there. I remember a conversation with an LDDC officer in 1988 in which he described the Isle of Dogs as a 'brownfield site'. The problem with this from my perspective was that more than 12,000 people lived there!

In Westminster, The Connection at St Martin's has done a remarkable job working with homeless people on the streets in our part of the city – getting to know them, gaining their trust and bringing them in to use the services that will help them gain greater self-respect and autonomy. The task given us by the Council was to eradicate sleeping on the streets, which was always unrealistic. Numbers were reduced substantially, but not to zero. The Council then decided that street-based services were supporting people to stay on the streets and so made the problem worse. They decided to limit services to homeless people to what is provided in centres.

National and local government policy in relation to street homelessness is a not very edifying mix of carrot and stick. Churches are communities of people committed to the love of God and the love of neighbour. What churches can offer is a model of community which demonstrates that we belong together and which gets us beyond looking at each other sideways. At their best, churches are inclusive communities where people meet across social boundaries.

One of my most memorable days at St Martin-in-the-Fields was in 1996 when I walked the youngest of our children to school in Soho. As we crossed Leicester Square one of the drunks shouted out, 'F*** off Vicar.' I cycled up to the Council of Christians and Jews on the Euston Road for a meeting with a Roman Catholic nun and a Jewish rabbi, and then to the Dorchester Hotel – they didn't know what to do with my bike, it would have been easier if I had arrived in a Rolls Royce! – to say Grace at a lunch which President Mandela was giving the Queen and hundreds of others during his state visit. In the afternoon I went to Wormwood Scrubs to visit a friend in prison and in the evening ran an education course at church.

That range of social experience is very unusual. People also experience it on the annual pilgrimage from St Martin's to Canterbury. On the Friday of the late May Bank Holiday weekend about 70 people set off from the steps of St Martin's. Over the course of the weekend others join them along the way. By the time we reach Canterbury Cathedral on Monday after-noon the number has grown to about 140. Sleeping on village hall floors, travelling light without the sorts of possessions that separate us and make it clear which social group we belong to, and walking 75 miles is like climbing Everest for some of us, so we need to help each other to make sure we arrive together.

In my first year I was walking with two men, both in jeans and T-shirt, absorbed in conversation as we walked through the Kent fields. Only after more than an hour did I discover that one was a university professor and one would be back on the streets that night having had his weekend's holiday. Ask anyone who becomes part of the St Martin's community and they will say that one of the things they value most about it is this sort of experience of community. None of us lives simply as individuals. We exist only in relationship, and the longing for community is a very deep one.

By extension, our work with homeless people in the twentieth century was originally funded by the BBC Christmas Appeal. The very first church service ever broadcast came from St Martin-in-the-Fields on 6 January 1924. Twice a year for the next three years the vicar would invite the extended congrega-tion to give to the collection. Lord Reith decided that this needed to be regularized and so 'The Week's Good Cause' was born and every year since 1927 the vicar of St Martin's has been allowed to make a Christmas Appeal on BBC Radio 4. It is an extraordi-nary event, with volunteers on the phones for the day and a small team of mostly elderly people opening the post for about three weeks. The year 2006 raised a miraculous £790,000, which was divided between our work in Trafalgar Square and a Relief Fund that each year helps more than 2,000 people in extreme need across the country. This Appeal is a marvellous example of about 7,000 listeners to Radio 4 responding to the needs of their neighbours.

Recently I was struck by a verse in Luke's Gospel in which Jesus said: 'The kings of the Gentiles lord it over them; and those in authority over them are called benefactors. But not so with you; rather the greatest among you must become like the youngest, and the leader like one who serves' (Luke 22.25–26). There is a great deal to be thankful for about charity and benefactors. That well of human kindness is what the daily work of organizations like St Martin-in-the-Fields depends on. Yet that vision of the kingdom of God gives something further to aim for which unsettles us in the present because it addresses the power relationships between us. What is looked for is relationships of reciprocity in which we discover what each has to give and receive, and in which relationships are not determined by money and social position.

In the past few years street homelessness has had unprecedented attention and some surprising alliances have emerged. A local hotel was exasperated by the rubbish generated by the rough sleepers at its back door. At a memorable meeting they discovered that the rough sleepers were equally fed up at being woken several times a night by well-meaning people bringing them food which was left beside them and became rubbish that attracted rats. The recognition of this common interest was one of the reasons which led government to fund the Salvation Army to co-ordinate and reduce the number of 'soup runs' to a level more appropriate to the needs of the current number of rough sleepers.

In this case homeless people themselves held the key to change as a common interest was found. It is in marked contrast to the shrill language of 'zero tolerance' used by those seeking to impose their power and who are inevitably frustrated by their lack of progress. The kingdom of God is a community in which we deal with our neighbour face to face and move beyond that sideways look at each other which is uncertain and typical of the way we currently look at poverty and homelessness.

CHAPTER 3

Good religion

We have a problem with religion

When the British Government was considering a new law against religious hatred which risked outlawing offensive religious jokes, the Christian website 'Ship of Fools' ran a competition to find the best God joke ever. The winner, from more than 20 years before, was by Emo Philips:

Once I saw this guy on a bridge about to jump.
I said, 'Don't do it!'
He said, 'Nobody loves me.'
I said, 'God loves you. Do you believe in God?'
He said, 'Yes.'
I said, 'Are you a Christian or a Jew?'
He said, 'A Christian.'
I said, 'Me, too! Protestant or Catholic?'
He said, 'Protestant.'
I said, 'Me, too! What franchise?'
He said, 'Baptist.'
I said, 'Me, too! Northern Baptist or Southern Baptist?'
He said, 'Northern Baptist.'
I said, 'Me, too! Northern Conservative Baptist or Northern Liberal Baptist?'
He said, 'Northern Conservative Baptist.'
I said, 'Me, too! Northern Conservative Baptist Great

Lakes Region, or Northern Conservative Baptist Eastern Region?'

He said, 'Northern Conservative Baptist Great Lakes Region.'

I said, 'Me, too! Northern Conservative Baptist Great Lakes Region Council of 1879, or Northern Conservative Baptist Great Lakes Region Council of 1912?'

He said, 'Northern Conservative Baptist Great Lakes Region Council of 1912.'

I said, 'Die, heretic!' And I pushed him over.[1]

If anyone had told me when I became Vicar of St Martin-in-the-Fields in 1995 that I would become an expert on creating liturgies after major acts of terrorism, I would not have believed them. None of us spotted then that major acts of terrorism would define the start of the twenty-first century. In our first few years of living in Trafalgar Square, London was experiencing the tail end of IRA bombing, one of the largest of which was in the parish I had just come from, on the Isle of Dogs, though a number of small bombs went off within 400 yards of our front door. What has happened at the start of this century has been on quite a different scale and its impact global. On the Sunday after '9/11' in 2001 we broadcast Sunday worship on BBC Radio 4. It seemed vital to involve an imam and a rabbi. Terrorism seeks to divide. We insisted on standing together. That set a pattern for other services. We assume there will be more.

In *Writing in the Dust*, some very personal reflections on having been caught up in the events in lower Manhattan on 11 September 2001, Rowan Williams, the Archbishop of Canterbury, memorably wrote:

We have had the chance to read the messages sent by passengers on the planes to their spouses and families in the desperate last minutes; and we have seen the spiritual advice apparently given to the terrorists by one of their number, the thoughts that should have been in their minds as they approached the death they had chosen (for themselves and for others). Something of the chill of 11 September 2001 lies in the contrast.

The religious words are, in the cold light of day, the words that murderers are saying to themselves to make a martyr's drama out of a crime. The non-religious words are testimony to what religious language is supposed to be about – the triumph of pointless, gratuitous love, the affirming of faithfulness even when there is nothing to be done or salvaged.

It should give us pause, especially if we think we are religious. You don't have to be Richard Dawkins to notice that there is a problem.[2]

We are in trouble with religion. What is good religion and how we discriminate good religion from bad are among the most pressing questions of our day.

How did we get here?

Throughout the twentieth century, but particularly since the Second World War, in Britain and western Europe there was a rapid process of secularization. Christianity has lost numbers and social and political significance. When I was training for ordination in the 1970s, the prevailing assumption in society was that religion had been in terminal decline since the Enlightenment and in the end all sensible people would grow out of it.

What became clear towards the end of the twentieth century is that religion is a persistent phenomenon and will not go away. In response to our 'brief moment in the sun' we human beings wonder at the beauty of creation and, in all the chaos and chances of our lives, at the enduring power of love. We long for relationship with God and with each other. To be human is to be religious.

Western secularization and a scientific outlook have not killed religion. Scientists are still agnostics, atheists *and* religious believers, in much the same proportion as in the population as a whole, but as the Church lost its hold over the majority of the population new religious movements multiplied, lots of them absurd. As G. K. Chesterton said at the beginning of the twentieth century, 'When people stop believing in God, it's not that they will believe in nothing but that they will believe in anything'. It is not difficult to see why Richard Dawkins thinks religion is like a virus that endangers humanity.

At the same time, one of the impacts of globalization is that we have become immediate neighbours to a world of faiths. Nowhere is this more apparent than in our great cities. London is now 'a world in a city' in which over 300 first languages are spoken and all the world's religions are present. The fabric of the city includes a striking variety of places of worship, some of which have changed hands with shifting local populations, like the Mosque in Brick Lane that used to be a synagogue but was originally a Huguenot church.

Because of the process of secularization, the increased emphasis on the individual and the privatization of religion, and the rapid rise in our awareness of religious pluralism, we now struggle with the critical questions about what makes for good religion or bad. It is striking how this lack of confidence has vacated the ground in such a way that over-confident minorities have claimed the territory as their own. We have become anxious about religion. Humour often deals with what we find otherwise almost impossible to handle. Our comedians play an important role in helping us to place our anxieties. Nevertheless, if religion is part of the problem, those of us with a religious faith had better try to find ways in which religion becomes part of the solution. An attempt to identify what makes for good religion is pressing.

Being fully human

Every religion carries an account of what it is to be human. To the extent that this is shared with others it might be described as universal wisdom, but each religion also has its own distinctive account. Christianity says that we are made in the image of God, are creative, intelligent and have a considerable degree of free choice and therefore moral responsibility. That's not exactly unique, but the recognition of Christ as the human face of God does show a distinctive pattern of service and sacrificial, faithful love that Christians would say is at the heart of what it is to be fully human.

Irenaeus, the second-century Bishop of Lyons, said that the glory of God is a person fully alive. That's a fair test of good religion. The critical question, not easily answered in an age preoccupied with self-realization and hedonism, is whether this Christian account makes us bigger people with larger hearts and minds; whether Christianity makes us more alive or less?

At the heart of the Christian gospel is the proclamation of Jesus for people to repent *for the forgiveness of sins*. The centrality of forgiveness in Christianity is vital to people turning round and starting again, but what is implied about human nature is not altogether welcome news. In the 1960s there was a reaction against such a negative account of our natures, particularly because so many of us are better at beating ourselves up for being bad people than at recognizing with delight the creative divine spark of our being made in the image of God. It seemed better to celebrate what is good, and hope that the bad would drop away.

The trouble is that this created a tendency not to take sin seriously. When I went to teach Ethics at Lincoln Theological

College in 1983 I made a survey of the eight introductory text-books then readily available in English, and found that five did not even include the word 'sin' in the index. Traditionally, evangelicals have held on better than liberals to the language of our being sinners in need of redemption. There is, of course, an age-old debate about whether forgiveness is a once-only or continuous process. Our being forgiven – 'Go and sin no more' – gets contrasted with how many times must I forgive and be forgiven? Not once, but seventy times seven. But it would be a dishonest Christian who claimed only to know about sin from the past or from the observation of others. We begin by assuming we are sinners seeking God's forgiveness. Good religion does not produce self-righteousness but repentance.

The Gospels contain stories of healing in fulfilment of what is known as 'the Isaiah agenda': 'the blind see, the lame walk, the lepers are cleansed, the deaf hear, the dead are raised and the poor have good news brought to them', read by Jesus at the synagogue in Nazareth (Luke 4.16–21). Good religion heals, and that Jesus does this is how he is revealed as the Messiah, the anointed one of God. What we glimpse in Christ is a vision of the kingdom of God that makes us restless and unsettled because we are no longer content with present realities: 'Thy kingdom come, on earth as in heaven'. Peace and justice, shalom, are our priority, and the end to which we align ourselves.

Our healing begins when we stop believing we can get it all sorted by ourselves and turn to God. I love the New English Bible's original translation of the first of the Beatitudes: 'Blessed are those who know their need of God' (Matthew 5.3). Such a person is open to God, and that's where healing begins. We find ourselves to be both under God's judgement and held by that indelible bond of baptism through which nothing can separate us from the love of God in Christ Jesus (Romans 8.39).

This is particularly important at present because of our profoundly disturbing apocalyptic fears. Some of these are new versions of an age-old drama about our elemental fears of chaos and evil. These are vividly portrayed in the massively hyped film, *Snakes on a Plane*. Snakes, archetypal evil, overrun a supposedly sealed and safe human-made environment. Human ingenuity and heroism see the passengers through, and that feels very good. Well, it takes your mind off the possibility of crashing or the threat of terrorism! Other apocalyptic fears strike me as new. For example, the fear of human-made climate chaos and our not knowing if we have the capacity or the time to act in any meaningful way that can save ourselves and the world. It may already be too late. Or another type of apocalyptic fear is of catastrophe completely beyond our control, such as a meteorite slamming into the earth and destroying us in probably the same way as dinosaurs were wiped out 60 million years ago. Fear creates paralysis and a sense of meaninglessness or worthlessness, but good religion helps people find what is needed for the repair, healing and transformation of the world.

One of the commonplace observations about Christianity is that the opposite of faith is not doubt but fear. You don't find faith without doubt, but Jesus' response to the disciples caught in a storm was 'O ye of little faith, why are ye fearful?' (Matthew 8.26). At its best, this gives Christianity a remarkable capacity to help people face reality, able to act by faith without the paralysis of fear. The stilling of the storm is a powerful metaphor for individuals and communities facing the more disturbing realities of our existence.

We are used to thinking about the healing of individuals, but the healing of societies is also our witness. The most obvious example is the process of largely non-violent change in South Africa and the use of the image of the rainbow nation, God's covenant with all creation. If Christianity was part of the problem, with the Dutch Reformed Church providing a theological rationale for apartheid, the Church was also part of the solution, finding the language of the rainbow covenant. Nowadays, in the entrance of South Africa House in Trafalgar Square, you are met by the two busts, of Oliver Tambo, father of the African National Congress and the 'new nation', and Archbishop Trevor Huddleston, father of the Anti-Apartheid movement. South Africa has given the world hope and delight in the rich variety of God's rainbow people.

The late Bishop John V. Taylor, whose formative missionary experience was in East Africa, preaching at St Martin-in-the-Fields a few years before he died, said that in Europe we have come to live by Descartes's 'I think, therefore I am', but in Africa being human is expressed as, 'I belong, therefore I am.' A Ugandan refugee on the Isle of Dogs wept at breakfast after the Easter ceremonies. She said, 'Now I can die in England because I know there will be people at my funeral.' She belonged. In South Africa, Archbishop Desmond Tutu translates the idea of '*ubuntu*' as 'a person is a person through a person'. When someone asks 'Are you well?', the response is 'I am well if you are well.'

For Christians, the deep experience of being fully alive is in our sharing in Christ's resurrection from the dead. This account draws us into the creation of a new community. Our well-being is with one another, a community of the resurrection. The stories of Jesus tell of this being a surprising community in which the outcast are welcome and where the rich and powerful should not assume they will be on the top table. This is a community in which humility is a virtue and in which people know their need of God and their incompleteness when even one is missing. This Christian experience witnesses to something universally true, that either we human beings learn to live together as one world or there will be no world.

If the Christian community is to offer anything to our diverse world we are going to have to learn to live together in a richly diverse communion *with conviction*. In communion we become fully human and hold a pearl of great price for the world. Not that you would think this from the way the Anglican communion is currently behaving, but I still believe it is part of our witness to the world, and part of what it means for good religion to make us more fully human.

Truth

One of the things I most admire from the recent history of St Martin's is the number of older members of the congregation who came searching for something and stayed, 'because it seemed so "real"'. It is difficult to make this an adequate test of religion, but there is a sense in which you know it when you meet it.

In a marvellous sermon preached at the annual service at Cambridge University to commemorate benefactors, the church historian Professor Eamon Duffy observed that they remember the powerful, 'and the very, very rich, who have shared their wealth – in many cases their loot – with [that] university'.[3] As an historian he said it is important not to edit out the inconvenient or disagreeable but to hold the tensions as they really are in a university (and a church) which is, at heart, 'about the truth'. 'About the truth' is a good phrase because philosophically there is uncertainty in the idea of absolute truth, but to say we are 'about the truth' makes a commitment that truth matters even though it is difficult both philosophically and in practice.

In a sustained attack on religion, Richard Dawkins wrote *The God Delusion*.[4] For Dawkins, all religion is bad religion, and religion is like a virus corrupting our human nature, preventing us from facing up to the truth. Much to my annoyance, I found myself thinking about Dawkins during Nine Lessons and Carols one Christmas. It was during the second reading, the one about the Fall, from the *second* creation story in Genesis, which in itself is a pretty good clue that what we are dealing with is not a scientific account of creation.

The man and the woman hid from the presence of the Lord God among the trees of the garden. When the Lord called the man, he said, 'I heard the sound of you in the garden, and I was afraid, because I was naked; and I hid myself.' I wondered whether Dawkins could describe in scientific terms anything like as well what it feels like to be human, having done something wrong and experiencing shame, guilt and blaming others.

There was a wonderfully strident attack on Dawkins by the Marxist Terry Eagleton, Professor of English Literature at Manchester University. It begins,

> Imagine someone holding forth on biology whose only knowledge of the subject is the *Book of British Birds*, and you have a rough idea of what it feels like to read Richard Dawkins on theology . . .
>
> Dawkins believes that all faith is blind faith, and that Christian and Muslim children are brought up to believe unquestioningly. Not even the dim-witted clerics who knocked me about at grammar school thought that. For mainstream Christianity, reason, argument and honest doubt have always played an integral role in belief.[5]

It's high time someone other than theologians took Dawkins to task for sloppy thinking, no matter how engaging a communicator he seems to be.

One of Dawkins' earliest and most interesting books is called *The Selfish Gene*.[6] Rowan Williams commented that the title is a sort of category mistake. Genes don't have self-consciousness, so how is it appropriate to call them selfish? Dawkins' point was that selfishness is built in to our nature as a survival strategy. Being human and gaining a sense of moral responsibility is to get beyond this and live not just for ourselves but with regard for others. According to Dawkins, this heightened sense of consciousness – which in Christianity is expressed by 'Do unto others as you would have them do to you' and 'Love your neighbour as yourself' – is good for our survival, so it, too, is enlightened self-interest and, in the end, essentially selfish.

Here, Dawkins seems entirely to miss an aspect of being human because of that crashing shift of gear in which he moves from a statement about evolutionary biology to one about moral philosophy. He assumes that, in the end, we are only self-interested, whereas other scientists at the moment emphasize not the selfishness of each species but our interdependence and the need for biodiversity: we need each other and one of our deepest fears is that human selfishness might be destroying the planet and our own chance for survival.

Christianity has a mixed history, but within it there has been a highly motivated and sustained attempt to seek the truth in the belief that God is truth. This search for truth is one of the touchstones of good religion.

Fruitfulness

Jesus said, 'By their fruits you will know them' and St Paul took the standard lists of virtues of his day and identified them as the fruits of the Spirit: 'love, joy, peace, patience, kindness, generosity, faithfulness, gentleness and self-control' (Galatians 5.22). So another test of good religion is whether it fosters what are universally perceived to be virtues. Does the practice of religion make us better people?

Contemporary Christianity is very comfortable in this area of moral virtue, but we might be cautious. First, Jesus was fantastically adept at undermining the morally superior and over-confident such as the rich young man who said he had kept all the commandments but just couldn't face giving away all his possessions, or the Pharisee praying in the temple, 'I thank thee O Lord that I am not like other men' in contrast to the publican, 'Lord have mercy on me a sinner.' Second, the heart of the gospel is to do with the forgiveness of sins and of our learning to forgive others as we have been forgiven. Jesus said that it is the person who has been forgiven much who will love much. It was Archbishop William Temple who said that the world will be transformed not by virtue but by love.

It is an easy critique of religion that so much damage and conflict can be laid at our feet. It is also the case that good religion moves people to do good. In this respect, St Martin-in-the-Fields holds something of a symbolic role within our national consciousness. In the twentieth century St Martin's became 'the church of the ever open door'; it was the place where Amnesty International was born in the mind of its founder; where Shelter grew from the meetings of six homelessness charities, including our own, meeting in the crypt after the broadcast of *Cathy Come Home* in 1966; the Anti-Apartheid movement found support for their vigil outside South Africa House in the church next door; and the *Big Issue* magazine was launched in our crypt. Then there is our own work caring for people in need, mostly in the UK but also internationally.

According to St Paul, the disciple of Christ is like an athlete in training, so we need to be disciplined in our religious practice. This isn't just about how we feel in the moment but about what we set our hopes on, what we strive for in our lives, and the habits we need to maintain. In a way this tests our commitment and determination, whether religion is sufficiently worth it as to make a long-term and not just a momentary commitment. Good religion sustains institutions that support people in their commitments: for example, marriage in the absence of perpetual honeymoon, and the family as the particular community in which we learn how to love. Their tried and tested purpose is to help sustain us as people who faithfully love in the long term. That, too, might be a test of fruitfulness, as might be the ability to create alternative structures that support love when the existing institutions fail us.

If something is 'real' it does not need to be defensive and can be open to dialogue that might change us. Increasingly, this is a touchstone for the Church. Are we open to the truth of the stranger in the way that Jesus suggested the kingdom of God is to be found in the marginal and disregarded?

In *God's Politics*[7] Jim Wallis, one of the leaders of the Sojourners community in Washington DC, suggested that there are two powerful forces in the world today: 'the hunger for spirituality and the passion for social change'. This is what 'real' religion does, like nothing else on earth. The trouble is, as G. K. Chesterton wryly observed 100 years ago, 'It's not that Christianity has been tried and found wanting but that it has been found difficult and not tried.'

Vision

Iris Murdoch wrote an essay with the marvellous title, 'Vision and Choice in Morality'.[8] Vision is what gives us a sense of other possible worlds. It makes us restless with what is unsatisfactory in the here and now. Jesus' vision of the kingdom of God is what Christians have set their hearts on and are restless for. We pray every day as Christ taught us for God's kingdom to come on earth as it is in heaven.

St Martin-in-the-Fields' 'Prayer for the World' is a commentary on that phrase of the Lord's Prayer. It is a civilized and civilizing prayer for the common good, recognizing duties and responsibilities for the poor, a longing for the very best of what it is to be human. It is an expression of the conviction that we only exist in community and that God's kingdom is not simply a private, individualistic matter:

O God, our Heavenly Father, give us a vision of our world as your love would make it: a world where the weak are protected and none go hungry or poor; a world where the benefits of civilized life are shared, and everyone can enjoy them; a world where different races, nations and cultures live in tolerance and mutual respect; a world where peace is built with justice, and justice is guided by love; and give us the inspiration and courage to build it, through Jesus Christ our Lord. Amen.

What Jesus gives is a vision that the kingdom of God is near at hand and for the good of all. This is very unsettling, but once you have glimpsed the possibilities of peace and justice you just can't settle for less, and any good religion must contain that sort of compelling vision energizing people to work for the coming of God's kingdom with all their heart and mind and strength. That we fail, or that we are inconsistent, is another matter altogether, revealing an aspect of what it is to be human. We all need a vision and to attempt to live in response to that vision.

Some years ago our neighbours at St James' Piccadilly used a slogan on one of their parish plans: 'A task without a dream is a drudge; a dream without a task is a chimera; a task and a dream is the hope of the world'.

An encounter with God

This may seem obvious, but above all, good religion must be an encounter with God. There's more to life than meets the eye, and a part of our human yearning is expressed in Michelangelo's painting on the ceiling of the Sistine Chapel of God reaching out to Adam and their fingers not quite touching. Good religion helps makes the connection near possible, paradoxically not by our own efforts.

Austen Williams, my predecessor but one as Vicar of St Martin's, kept on his desk a handwritten copy of the poem 'Final Instructions' by his friend Cecil Day-Lewis. It is about the artist

but it could almost equally well be about the priestly encounter
with God:

> For sacrifice, there are certain principles –
> Few, but essential.
>
> I do not mean your ritual. This you have learnt –
> The garland, the salt, a correct use of the knife,
> And what to do with the blood:
> Though it is worth reminding you that no two
> Sacrifices ever turn out alike –
> Not where this god is concerned.
>
> The celebrant's approach may be summed up
> In three words – patience, joy,
> Disinterestedness. Remember, you do not sacrifice
> For your own glory or peace of mind:
> You are there to assist the clients and please the god.
>
> It goes without saying
> That only the best is good enough for the god.
> But the best – I must emphasize it – even your best
> Will by no means always be found acceptable.
> Do not be discouraged:
> Some lizard or passing cat may taste your sacrifice
> And bless the god: it will not be entirely wasted.
>
> But the crucial point is this:
> You are called only to *make* the sacrifice:
> Whether or no he enters into it
> Is the god's affair; and whatever the handbooks say,
> You can neither command his presence nor explain it –
> All you can do is to make it possible.

If the sacrifice catches fire of its own accord
On the altar, well and good. But do not
Flatter yourself that discipline and devotion
Have wrought the miracle: they have only allowed it.

So luck is all I can wish you, or need wish you.
And every time you prepare to lay yourself
On the altar and offer again what you have to offer,
Remember, my son,
Those words – patience, joy, disinterestedness.[9]

Reasonable belief

We are plagued by 'bad' religion and it threatens the world. I went out into Trafalgar Square on a day when hundreds of people were enjoying being at the centre of London in summer sunshine. A Christian evangelist with a loudspeaker berated us for our sinfulness. No one listened, and by our not listening the inference was drawn that we were rejecting God and would be going to hell. It seemed a very long way from the engaging story-teller from Nazareth whom the crowds came to listen to in their thousands and who gave them food, healing and life in all its fullness.

It would be a mistake comparable to that of Richard Dawkins' dogmatic atheism to suggest that all religion is good religion. There is a lot of religious rubbish around and it can be lethally dangerous. That is why so many organizations exclude religious purposes from their charitable funding. They will fund good work done by religious groups, but they simply do not know how else to distinguish good religion from bad, as this chapter has attempted to begin to do.

Comedians have no such difficulty. They might be signposting a way through this problem by identifying the usual criteria of reasonableness and coherence that make for good and bad in anything. This chapter began with a joke, so it is going to end with one as well, which is my favourite religious joke at the moment. Unlike the earlier one, I have no idea who deserves to be credited for it, except that I first heard it from my colleague and Associate Vicar, Liz Griffiths. It is a simple way of saying that good religion matters and bad religion contains the seeds of our destruction.

An atheist was walking through the woods. As he walked, he said to himself, 'What majestic trees! What powerful rivers! What beautiful animals!' Alongside the river, he heard a rustling in the bushes behind him. He turned to look and saw a seven-foot grizzly bear charging towards him. He ran as fast as he could up the path. He looked over his shoulder and seeing that the bear was closing in on him, he stumbled and fell to the ground. Rolling over, he saw that the bear was right on top of him, reaching for him with his left paw and raising his right paw to strike him. At that instant the atheist cried out, 'Oh my God!' Time stopped. The bear froze. The forest was silent. A bright light shone upon the man, and a voice from above said, 'You deny my existence for all these years, teach others I don't exist and even credit creation to cosmic accident. Do you expect me to help you out of this predicament?' The atheist looked directly into the light. 'I recognize that it would be hypocritical of me suddenly to ask you to treat me as a Christian now,' the atheist said, 'but perhaps you could make the bear a Christian?' There was a pause. 'OK,' said the voice. The light shining down on them went out, the sun shone and the sounds of the forest resumed, with the birds singing and the brook babbling. And slowly the bear dropped his right paw, bowed his head and brought both paws together to pray, saying, 'Lord bless this food, which you have provided out of your bounty. Amen'.

CHAPTER 4

This is the age of many stories

When a small group of Anglican Franciscans moved into Whitechapel in east London in the early 1980s they introduced themselves to their neighbours. The news that they prayed four times a day was met with blank incomprehension by the white east-enders on one side, but the Bengali Muslims on the other side smiled and said, 'Ah, that's like us, only we pray five times a day'. London is 'a world city' in religious terms as well as culturally, economically and politically. The lively presence of other faiths has awakened a wider interest in religion. Once again, faith matters.

Once upon a time there may have been a single story for the whole community to interpret their experience and find meaning. A thousand years ago, at the beginning of the last millennium, in western Europe, the Bible was understood as a single over-arching narrative from Genesis to Revelation, which provided the framework within which all human life was understood and interpreted. This single biblical narrative was the means by which people of every age could find reality and meaning. The world could only be understood in terms of this single biblical epic; indeed, in a way it shaped people's experience of reality.

This view of things began to break down under the pressure of exploration – both geographic exploration through which people came into contact with different epic stories in other parts of the world, and intellectual exploration, particularly science, which gave alternative accounts of life. It isn't possible to live in a city like London without being aware of these varied and sometimes competing stories. They are religious *and* secular, and one of the key differences between people is to do with how we respond to this diversity, this pluralism. As Arundhati Roy said in her novel *The God of Small Things*,[1] it is no longer possible for us to tell one story, 'this is the age of many stories'. In a world in which religion fuels some of the great conflicts, the question of how these stories sit side by side, and whether we can pray together, is pressing.

One kind of religious response is to turn in on your own community and put up walls between yourself or your community and the rest of the world with its competing or different and often uncomfortable stories. The current temptation is to see this as a problem for Islam, but Christians know it in the extraordinary rise of 'Creationism', an ideology declining the insights, but not the benefits, of science. Among Jews the Meir Shearim, the ultra-Orthodox area of Jerusalem, is a geographic area where people dress in the style of the eighteenth century and hold on to their view of the world by living a separated life which gives that community a strong sense of meaning and purpose over against the challenges and limitations of the modern world.

A similar contemporary mindset can be found in some of the new Jewish settlements on the West Bank. At one I visited in 1998 a highly articulate and rather frightening American Jewish immigrant to Israel passionately explained the Jewish entitlement to settle the land with no recognition of the at least equal claim of the Palestinians who had been living there before them. One of the group I was with from the Council of Christians and Jews, a minister from Belfast, said he found it an all too familiar story. Indeed, the Church has a long track record of living in a similar way, putting up the sort of barriers that protect our exclusive version of truth. You can find it in every religious faith.

On the Sunday after 9/11, we broadcast *Sunday Worship* on BBC Radio 4 from St Martin's. Rabbi Mark Winer and the late Dr Zaki Badawi prayed with me and we realized that the threat was not from 'other faiths' but from fundamentalism and that turning inwards which refused to engage creatively with difference. A lovely verse from the First Letter of John in the New Testament offers a way forward: 'Perfect love casts out fear' (1 John 4.18).

In January 1998, on the fiftieth anniversary of Gandhi's assassination, the actor Ben Kingsley, who played Gandhi in Richard Attenborough's biopic, stood in the pulpit of St Martin-in-the-Fields. He read from the writings of the Mahatma or 'great soul'. At the end he added unexpectedly: 'When I despair, I remember that all through history the way of truth and love has always won. There have been tyrants, and for a time they have seemed invincible, but in the end they always fall. Think of it, *always*.' I was struck with such force that I felt impelled to go in search of Gandhi first in books and then by physically making a journey to an ashram at Sevagram in the centre of India where Gandhi had lived for 15 years. There were still a number of people there who had lived with him. At this ashram the day was framed by prayers at 4.30 in the morning and 5.30 in the afternoon on spacious ground open to the sky and to the poorest of the poor. The recitation of prayers included the Lord's Prayer, which was the 22nd in a compilation of 26 from the world's major religious traditions. While staying at Sevagram, I met a Hindu holy man travelling (by which I mean walking) throughout India in the cause of 'cow protection' who told me that he was a follower of Jesus *and* a Hindu. The ashram was united by an ethical universalism which claimed that all religions are united in their attention to truth, love, service, self-control and social discipline. I was grateful for the immense respect they had for me as a Christian and for all people of different faiths. A wonderful spirit was there, a breath of fresh air.

In Attenborough's film there was a clergyman called C. F. Andrews. He has become one of my Christian heroes. He was one of the great explorers charting a way of being faithful to Christ in this world of faiths. Andrews was a missionary who travelled to India in 1904 to join the Cambridge Brotherhood in Delhi. He was 33 years old and had been a Christian priest teaching at Cambridge University. He loved the Lord Jesus and he wanted to take his faith and share it with people who did not yet know Christ. He took with him a Sanskrit dictionary, and from the start it was obvious that he wanted to engage with Indian culture. In later life he looked back on 20 March 1904, the day he set foot in India for the first time, as a second birthday. It cut his life in two and made him, in the languages of North India a *dwija*, a twice born. Almost exactly half his life was lived in the West and half in the East.

In Delhi he quickly made a close friendship with a gentle, saintly Muslim, a Sufi mystic, called Zaka Ullah. They met frequently to talk about religion, but never to try to convert the other. 'What is the use of argument and controversy?' asked Zaka Ullah. 'You tell me your Beautiful Names for God, and I will tell you mine.'

Similarly, Andrews made friends with holy Sikhs and Hindus and discovered how they could talk about the deeper things of religion, as lovers of God. Charlie Andrews had a large heart, but his ability to engage with other faiths came out of the largeness of his Christianity. He wrote, 'Because Christ is Son *of Man*, Christianity must be all-comprehensive, larger far than the church of the baptized. The Christian experience must be one of an all-embracing sacrament, in which Christ is seen and revered in all men.' He lived a very simple life and worked as a schoolteacher and stands out as one of the giants of his time. He was asked by Indian friends to go to South Africa to support the Indian community which was being systematically oppressed. There he met a young Indian lawyer, Mohandes K. Gandhi, and their friendship flourished for a lifetime. Andrews wrote of an evening when Gandhi sat under the open sky nursing a sick child on his lap, a little Muslim boy. Next to him was a Christian Zulu girl. Gandhi read some Gujarati verses about the love of God and explained them in English. Gujarati hymns were then sung by the children. Gandhi asked Andrews to sing the Christian hymn 'Lead kindly light' as the darkness grew deeper, and in the silence that followed Gandhi repeated the last lines which spoke of hope at a time of darkness:

> And with the morn those angel faces smile,
> Which I have loved long since, and lost awhile.

It's one of those strange things about the meeting between different faiths that you learn not just about the other faith but about your own. You learn what you mean by things that you had taken for granted but not properly understood. You have to find out what is essential and what does not really matter. Sometimes the person of a different faith can teach you about your own. In Richard Attenborough's film there is an extraordinary scene when Andrews and Gandhi were walking along the street in South Africa. Pushed off the pavement by some white Boers, Gandhi asked Andrews about the teaching of Jesus to turn the other cheek in the face of violence. Andrews said that our Lord was speaking metaphorically. 'No,' said Gandhi, 'I think he meant what he said.'

By 1913, Charlie Andrews felt himself increasingly called to study Indian thought and interpret it to the West. He also wanted to try to express Christian thought to the East but from an independent standpoint, not as a paid agent like a priest and missionary. His Indian friends urged him not to be hasty but to wait for an unmistakable sign that this was the right thing to do. It came unexpectedly in a book by another Christian missionary, Albert Schweitzer's *The Quest of the Historical Jesus*.[2] The last paragraph so met Andrews' need that it became his favourite Christian quotation:

> Christ comes to us as One Unknown, without a name, just as of old by the lakeside He came to those men who knew Him not. He speaks to us the same words, 'Follow thou Me', and sets us to those tasks which He has to fulfil for our time. He commands. And to those who obey Him, whether they be wise or simple, He will reveal Himself in the toils, the conflicts, the sufferings, which they shall pass through in His fellowship. And as an ineffable mystery they shall learn in their own experience who He is.

These words seemed to free him to serve Jesus, this mysterious stranger, in the needs of Indian people and to find him in the richness of Indian religions. In the teaching of the Buddha he saw ancient calm serenity and that old age is reached with ripe wisdom. But he also found that the youthful Christ provided the world with a startlingly original and passionate challenge, 'the most revolutionary religious thinker whom the world has ever seen'.

In his later years, it was John's Gospel that C. F. Andrews loved and used most. According to John, the commandment to love in Jesus' teaching is linked with the friendship God offers us in Jesus:

> Jesus said, 'This is my commandment, that you love one another as I have loved you. No one has greater love than this, to lay down one's life for one's friends. You are my friends if you do what I command you. I do not call you servants any longer, because the servant does not know what the master is doing; but I have called you friends, because I have made known to you everything that I have heard from my Father. You did not choose me but I chose

you. And I appointed you to go and bear fruit, fruit that will last, so that the Father will give you whatever you ask him in my name. I am giving you these commands so that you may love one another.' (John 15.12–17)

Charlie Andrews had the most extraordinary capacity for friendships with Gandhi and the Bengali poet Rabindranath Tagore and with hundreds of children whom he taught and people he met in the cause of Indian nationalism. He also made deep friendships with some of the English colonials who were honest and good-hearted and open to his extraordinary spirit. He signed his letters, 'With affection, C. F. Andrews'.

One of the most striking things for a Westerner going to India now is that religion is all around. In the West we find it difficult to believe in God; in India it seems impossible not to. In 1940, at the end of C. F. Andrews' life, Gandhi travelled to Calcutta to visit him in hospital. I was astonished to discover that in his last words to Gandhi, Charlie Andrews repeated some lines from the English poet Francis Thompson's 'In No Strange Land'. They are about the way the religious is all around us, among us, inseparable from us:

> Does the fish soar to find the ocean,
> The eagle plunge to find the air,
> That we ask of the stars in motion
> If they have rumour of Thee there?

These last words of C. F. Andrews to Gandhi come from a poem that is almost certainly about St Martin-in-the-Fields which was no strange land for Francis Thompson, an opium addict who was taken in by a churchwarden of St Martin's, pitched, as Thompson says in that same poem, 'betwixt Heaven and Charing Cross'.

The purpose of religious dialogue is not to find an agreed

lowest common denominator but to share truth as best we see it. To say that God is real and that in Jesus we see God truly and fully in human form is not the same as to say that we have nothing more to learn about God. The language of the Trinity suggests that God is complex, like a person only infinitely more so, multifaceted and ultimately beyond our understanding. The scriptures say that the Holy Spirit will lead us into truth and that is the journey Christians seek to make by following in the way of Jesus Christ.

What gives me hope is that people who are secure in their own faith can have the largeness of heart of C. F. Andrews to engage in careful religious dialogue. In doing so we often discover a great deal about our own religious faith as well as about the faith of others. We learn what is held in common and that there are some interesting and often creative differences, which is what we would expect given the great variety of humanity under one God. As long as it is God we attend to with care and reverence, living in this age of many stories is exhilarating.

CHAPTER 5

The art of the Bible

The Bible is the world's Number 1 best seller. It has shaped the lives of the rich and powerful as well as of people who have nothing. It has an astonishing capacity to fire and enliven, as well as to judge and purify. Time after time it changes the lives of individuals and communities. According to Isaiah, 'God's word shall not return empty but will accomplish and succeed in its purpose' (Isaiah 55.11). The Bible is a collection of 66 books written across a period of 1,000 years. Their Godliness is presented to us in a wonderful variety of literary styles: history and story, myth and allegory, poetry and imagery, prayer and praise.

Yet the Bible is also one of the most abused books in the world. It can be used unthinkingly by those who are not prepared to grapple with reality and who exhibit the worst of Christianity as people with soft heads and hard hearts. The Bible exists to point us to God, not to itself. Look at the different ways it has been used over the centuries and you will find challenges to the present drive for conformity.

The Lindisfarne Gospels were the product of one of the greatest and holiest centres of Christianity in Celtic Britain. Yet Lindisfarne, a small island off the Northumbrian coast, in the eighth century was a strange and distant world. Few people then had the education to read, and the beautiful highly decorated Gospels would have been displayed on the altars of Lindisfarne as well as in places like Chester-le-Street and Durham. Just a glimpse of the book could have changed a pilgrim's life. It had the power to heal body and soul.

It is hard to think of the later Protestant reformers, with their emphasis on the centrality of the words of scripture, being content with this visual and symbolic use of the unread book. To the Protestant mind, thinking that the power of Christ lay in our just looking at the Gospels smacks of superstition, a bit like keeping the family Bible in the bottom of the wardrobe unread but much loved. What seeing the Lindisfarne Gospels alerted me to was the very different ways in which the Bible has been understood and used down the ages. Yet always the text is there to point beyond itself to the mystery of the eternal God in time.

One of the greatest privileges about being the Vicar of St Martin-in-the-Fields is to be the parish priest of the National Gallery, one of our neighbours in Trafalgar Square. I love this partly because the members of the first confirmation class I ever took as a curate in Stepney in 1980 were not very good at reading. I struggled with how to engage them with the Bible. I bought some wonderful comic-strip books with titles like *Moses Desert Commander* and an excellent similar series of New Testament stories. Then I hit on the idea that the National Gallery had a lot of pictures of biblical scenes and wondered whether my group of young people could cope with the cultural leap involved in looking at some of the great art of western Europe. We visited the Gallery and much to my surprise they seemed to accept it as no stranger than anything else presented to them by church. In looking at two paintings of the nativity we explored the difference between Luke's and Matthew's Gospels with their different pictures of Jesus. We asked questions of the paintings and the text about what is a Gospel and what the evangelists were saying to us today. As for many clergy all over the country, I found that slides and postcards of these great paintings were a wonderful way of exploring the scriptures. Now I have the great good fortune of living opposite the National Gallery.

I know almost nothing about painting and the history of art, but the Gallery has a superbly well-equipped staff and it has been a pleasure to learn from them. With the encouragement and involvement of the then Director, Neil MacGregor, we began to explore the interplay of art and theology in a series of double acts: one of the Gallery staff would talk about a picture, I would read the biblical text that went with it, talk about the text and we would open a conversation about the painting and the text.

The first time we did this was in Lent 1997. We looked at two pictures a week following the way of the cross through the Gallery. St Martin's used to get 40 or so for Lent courses but that year for these Gallery talks we had between 120 and 180. For Neil MacGregor they were confirmation of the Gallery's plans for its millennium exhibition, *Seeing Salvation*. For me the series was a gift, engaging a church and wider audience with the biblical text and through these great paintings with the things of God. The paintings helped us to read the scriptures in a more attentive way.

We have done this many times since, even on the radio with listeners having to visualize the paintings with only the help of brief descriptions. This has been so enjoyable that I hope it will work in print even without the three pictures in front of you, exploring Christianity in a visual way, just like the youngsters in Stepney nearly 30 years ago.

'The Adoration of the Kings' by Jan Gossaert, painted 1510–15

The Adoration is one of the most sumptuous ever painted. It is thought to have been an altarpiece of the Lady Chapel of St Adrian's, Grammont, endowed by Johannes de Broeder, who became Abbot in 1506 . . . Every inch of the huge panel has been elaborated in dazzlingly crisp detail, without compromising the clarity and focus of the whole.[1]

The four Gospels begin in very different ways. Mark goes straight to the ministry of the adult Jesus: 'The beginning of the gospel of Jesus Christ, the Son of God'. John identifies Jesus with the creative Word of God and sets him in the context of creation: 'In the beginning was the Word . . .' Only Matthew and Luke have nativity stories. With the Stepney confirmation group I used Rembrandt's shepherds in the Dutch barn to explore Luke's Gospel. For Matthew we used this sumptuous adoration of the kings by Gossaert. Matthew didn't refer to these travellers as kings: he called them magi or wise men, from the East, probably from Persia, modern Iran. And he didn't say there were three of them, just that they brought three gifts. It wasn't until Tertullian in the second century that anyone thought of them as kings, and no one named them as Caspar, Melchior and Balthazar until the ninth century when these kings came to represent the three parts of the known world: Europe, Africa and Asia – kings of the earth worshipping the infant king of all. In the picture, as in the Gospel, the beginning of the Gospel is being used to help us see what sort of a Christ Jesus will be.

In the ruin of the old dispensation the kings came in adoration of the infant king. Dressed in clothes to die for, the height of Netherlandish fashion, they brought their gifts of gold, frankincense and myrrh. It wasn't until the fourth century that a hymn by Prudentius identified the symbolism of the gifts telling us who Christ is: gold for a king, frankincense for God and myrrh to embalm him when he died.

There are people looking at what has happened but it needs explaining because it is so unexpected. The sacrifice of Isaac is carved in a frieze high above the Virgin, to help us understand the father sacrificing his son out of obedience and love. The Gallery's guide says Joseph is looking to heaven, but to me he looks anxious, and that at least is not surprising.

The angelic host is impressive and the sky is alight with a new dawn, or is it that this light in the middle of the night is the opposite of what happened in the middle of the day on Good Friday when there was darkness at noon?

The dogs in the foreground are state-of-the-art copies from Dürer's engraving of the miraculous conversion of St Eustace, painted 1500/1. One has dug up and is gnawing a bone, the old Adam contrasted with our new nature being presented to us in Christ.

It's a wonderfully three-dimensional picture. The corridors in which Christ is presented go both deep into the picture and upwards to heaven. A dove, just below the top arch, and the star above that, show Jesus within the Trinity of God the Father, Son and Holy Spirit. The corridor into the depth of the picture has a donkey this side of a narrow gate, half open with a city across fields behind. The donkey is eating, its head down to the floor, showing the cross on its back. He is waiting to carry Christ into the city and on to the Passion at the heart of the Gospel. This painting is a brilliant example of how the whole Gospel can be seen in a single view. The text is similar:

In the time of King Herod, after Jesus was born in Bethlehem of Judea, wise men from the East came to Jerusalem, asking, 'Where is the child who has been born king of the Jews? For we observed his star at its rising, and have come to pay him homage.' When King Herod heard this, he was frightened, and all Jerusalem with him; and calling together all the chief priests and scribes of the people, he inquired of them where the Messiah was to be born. They told him, 'In Bethlehem of Judea; for so it has been written by the prophet:

"And you, Bethlehem, in the land of Judah, are by no means least among the rulers of Judah; for from you shall come a ruler who is to shepherd my people Israel."'

Then Herod secretly called for the wise men and learned from them the exact time when the star had appeared. Then

he sent them to Bethlehem, saying, 'Go and search dili-
gently for the child; and when you have found him, bring
me word so that I may also go and pay him homage.' When
they had heard the king, they set out; and there, ahead of
them, went the star that they had seen at its rising, until it
stopped over the place where the child was. When they saw
that the star had stopped, they were overwhelmed with joy.
On entering the house, they saw the child with Mary his
mother; and they knelt down and paid him homage. Then,
opening their treasure-chests, they offered him gifts of gold,
frankincense, and myrrh. And having been warned in a
dream not to return to Herod, they left for their own
country by another road. (Matthew 2.1–12)

This story is part of the Gospel's prologue in which Matthew is
giving us the eyes and ears to hear and see Jesus. There is so
much being offered us that it is worth looking at the whole
prologue.

Matthew 1.1–18

Other people's genealogies can be tedious but in this genealogy
Matthew is making some extraordinarily important points for
us. He traces Jesus' lineage to Abraham, the founder of Israel,
not to Adam, from whom everyone is descended, as in Luke.
Matthew's is the most Jewish Gospel, Luke's the most Greek. In
Matthew, salvation comes from Israel but the story of the magi
shows the end of the Gospel. After the resurrection, Jesus will
send the disciples to 'go and make disciples of all nations'. In
Matthew, Jesus' earthly ministry is confined to the Jews, with
two exceptions, both of which are explained with reference to
the Jews – the healing of the Canaanite woman (even the dogs
eat the crumbs from the table) and the Roman centurion (never
in Israel is there such faith).

The four women mentioned in this genealogy reveal much that is surprising about the ways of God. As Matthew's genealogy is in the form of a poem, the biblical scholar Michael Goulder suggested that the best way to comment on it might be in a poem:

> Exceedingly odd is the means by which God
> Has provided our path to the heavenly shore
> Of the girls from whose line the true light was to shine.
> There was one an adulteress, another a whore.
> There was Tamar who bore what we all should deplore
> A fine pair of twins to her father in law,
> And Rahab the harlot, her sins were as scarlet,
> As red as the thread that she hung from the door,
> Yet alone of her nation she came to salvation
> And lived to be mother of Boaz of yore,
> And he married Ruth, a gentle uncouth,
> In a manner quite counter to biblical lore,
> And of her there did spring David the King
> Who walked on his palace one evening and saw
> The wife of Uriah, from whom he did sire
> A baby that died – yes, and princes a score:
> And a mother unmarried it was too that carried
> God's son, and laid him in a manger of straw,
> That the moral might wait at the heavenly gate
> While the sinners and publicans go in before
> Who have not earned their place, but received it by grace,
> And have found them a righteousness not of the law.[2]

Matthew 1.18–25

Given that most Jews would reject Jesus, Matthew was keen to show how Jesus the Messiah was in fulfilment of the scriptures. Joseph's concerns about his betrothed becoming

67

pregnant are answered in a dream by an angel, and Matthew states that

> All this took place to fulfil what had been spoken by the Lord through the prophet [Isaiah 7.14]:
> 'Look, the virgin shall conceive and bear a son,
> And they shall name him Emmanuel'.

For those of us who are not Jewish and lack Hebrew, he helpfully adds, 'which means "God is with us"'.

This establishes one of Matthew's main themes: Jesus is the most surprising Messiah, but go back to the scriptures and you will find it is all there. Later in the main section of the Gospel, Matthew draws on Isaiah's suffering servant in order to understand Jesus. These texts had never been associated in Judaism with the expectation of the Messiah, and the link is quite astonishing. No wonder so many Jews didn't get it. Their leaders let them down: 'They were like sheep without a shepherd.'

Matthew 2.1–12

The magi travelled to Jerusalem in search of the child who had been born king of the Jews. King Herod was frightened but the chief priests and scribes were able to direct the travellers correctly to little Bethlehem on the basis of scripture. Evoking that sense of David being the youngest of Jesse's sons yet the one who would slay Goliath and become a great king, Bethlehem might seem to be much less significant than Jerusalem, but it is as foretold by the prophet Micah:

> And you, Bethlehem, in the land of Judah,
> are by no means least among the rulers of Judah;
> for from you shall come a ruler
> who is to shepherd my people Israel.

Jesus is going to be a king even greater than David. Like Joseph, the magi were warned in a dream and made their journey home without returning to Jerusalem to inform Herod.

Matthew 2.13–15

And the Holy Family fled into Egypt. If the birth in Bethlehem suggests that Jesus is going to a king even greater than David, then the flight into Egypt suggests that he is going to be even greater than Moses, and of course the whole Gospel hinges on the keeping of the Passover meal that leads into Good Friday and Easter Day.

Pay attention to the beginning of this Gospel, look closely at this picture, and you can see just who is being held before us by his mother. The picture is about neither the historical Jesus nor the Christ of ancient text, but the Christ of present faith. The infant sits on the Virgin's lap as if enthroned and the cup of gold coins is like a chalice, the coin that the infant holds like a eucharistic host. This was an altarpiece and here at the centre is a direct visual connection with the eucharistic elements being held before it by the priest.

'The Supper at Emmaus' by Caravaggio, painted 1601

Perhaps no great artist is as well documented in police records as Michelangelo Merisi, the painter from Caravaggio in Lombardy, who stalked the streets with a sword at his side, threw a plate of artichokes at a waiter, fought a duel and killed a man. He subsequently fled to Rome, joined the Knights of Malta, insulted a superior, escaped from prison, was disfigured by hired thugs, and died of a malignant fever at Port Ercole while the ship taking him to Rome and a Papal pardon sailed on with his belongings on board. There were those who saw in Caravaggio's dark paintings a reflection of his life. Some thought he had come to destroy art with his depiction of saints as coarse contemporary proletarians. Yet the truth must have been more complicated.[3]

According to Colin Wiggins from the Gallery's education department, 'Caravaggio was the Damian Hirst of his day.'

'The Supper at Emmaus' is one of my favourite pictures. A copy of it used to hang on the staircase in St Luke's School on the Isle of Dogs, courtesy of a Sainsbury's Trust initiative when the National Gallery's Sainsbury wing opened. If 'The Adoration of the Kings' is a depiction of the whole Gospel, Caravaggio's painting is a moment, an instant. The central figure is blessing the food on the table, which includes broken bread and wine. One second earlier and the two disciples hadn't recognized him, one second later and Jesus would be gone. The disciples are startled, the elbow of the figure on the left pokes through a hole in the cloth, and it also seems to push through the canvas into our space.

Now on that same day two of them were going to a village called Emmaus, about seven miles from Jerusalem, and talking with each other about all these things that had happened. While they were talking and discussing, Jesus himself came near and went with them, but their eyes were kept from recognizing him. And he said to them, 'What are you discussing with each other while you walk along?' They stood still, looking sad. Then one of them, whose name was Cleopas, answered him, 'Are you the only stranger in Jerusalem who does not know the things that have taken place there in these days?' He asked them, 'What things?' They replied, 'The things about Jesus of Nazareth, who was a prophet mighty in deed and word before God and all the people, and how our chief priests and leaders handed him over to be condemned to death and crucified him. But we had hoped that he was the one to redeem Israel. Yes, and besides all this, it is now the third day since these things took place. Moreover, some women of our group astounded us. They were at the tomb early this morning, and when they did not find his body there, they came back and told us that they had indeed seen a vision of angels who said that he was alive. Some of those who were with us went to the tomb and found it just as the women had said; but they did not see him.' Then he said to them, 'Oh, how foolish you are, and how slow of heart to believe all that the prophets have declared! Was it not necessary that the Messiah should suffer these things and then enter into his glory?' Then beginning with Moses and all the prophets, he interpreted to them the things about himself in all the scriptures.

As they came near the village to which they were going, he walked ahead as if he were going on. But they urged him strongly, saying, 'Stay with us, because it is almost evening and the day is now nearly over.' So he went in to stay with them.

When he was at the table with them, he took bread, blessed and broke it, and gave it to them. Then their eyes were opened, and they recognized him; and he vanished from their sight. They said to each other, 'Were not our hearts burning within us while he was talking to us on the road, while he was opening the scriptures to us?' That same hour they got up and returned to Jerusalem; and they found the eleven and their companions gathered together. (Luke 24.13–33)

The central question of the text is why the disciples did not recognize their companion. Caravaggio answers that problem by depicting Christ without a beard. For Luke it is more that the disciples need it all explaining yet again. The stranger on the road goes through it all again, 'beginning with Moses and all the prophets'.

There is a wonderful still life on the table, much of it with

71

symbolic significance: a roast chicken and a basket of fruit, just over-ripe and about to tip off the table. It makes the shadow of a fish on the cloth, a Christian symbol, the Greek word for fish being a mnemonic for 'Jesus Christ God's Son Saviour'. The scallop shell worn by the disciple on the right is the sign of a pilgrim to Compostella, the Christian life in the resurrection being a journey on the road to Emmaus, back to Jerusalem and on to the ends of the earth.

The light source in the painting is from outside as well as from Christ himself. The waiter, whose shadow does not darken the face of Christ, seems not to have seen anything strange, whereas the two disciples are startled. Seeing Christ is a matter of faith.

There is a 'Now you see him, now you don't' quality of the resurrection stories, which is particularly striking in Luke. His account of the resurrection takes place in the one day, in and around Jerusalem: the empty tomb and Mary Magdalene in the garden, the road to Emmaus, the appearance to the 11, the final teaching and the ascension. It is the end of the Gospel that leads into Luke volume 2, the Acts of the Apostles and the life of the early Church.

With Christ and the two disciples, there is space on the viewer's side of the table which is open for us as we, too, recognize the Lord in the blessing and breaking of bread. This, too, is a painting that invites us in faith to meet Christ in the Eucharist.

'The *Fighting Temeraire* Tugs to Her Last Berth to be Broken Up' by J. M. Turner, painted 1838

This is one of the nation's favourite paintings and takes us in to very different territory and a non-biblical painting. It is a meditation on change and death, grief and bereavement, which for many people are a test of their faith.

Turner was the son of a modest barber in Covent Garden, so very local to both St Martin's and the National Gallery. The

Fighting Temeraire was a 98-gun warship from Nelson's navy built of 5,000 oaks and manned by 750 sailors. The National Gallery, in Trafalgar Square with Nelson's column at its centre, could not be a more fitting home for it.

The sunset in the picture evokes the end of life, but so does the pallid hue of the old ship, like pale skin thin against its skeleton. The age of the sailing ship has gone. It is being towed up the Thames by a little tug, its funnel steaming and paddles turning. They are going to the breaker's yard at Rotherhithe, just across the river from the Isle of Dogs.

This is a painting about the passing from one age to another. The picture honours the great ship with a great past. That is a secure judgement. The future is less certain. Many in Turner's day saw the little tug as sinister, dirty and malevolent. Nowadays people seem more willing to see it positively. The new age harnesses energy more effectively and brings opportunities undreamt of by the previous generation. For us there is a romanticism about the age of steam as well as of sail.

That we will die is as certain as our changing world. Burying the dead, we praise their great lives and many achievements. It is a different world now, and the passing from one generation to another is an act of faith.

A favourite prayer for funerals and memorial services comes from a sermon preached by John Henry Newman. It was preached at St Nicholas', Littlemore, just outside Oxford, on 19 February 1843, as Newman was preparing to leave the Church of England and become a Roman Catholic. From just five years after this painting, it is a perfect prayer to accompany the picture:

> May He support us all the day long, till the shades lengthen, and the evening comes, and the busy world is hushed, and the fever of life is over, and our work done! Then in his mercy may He give us a safe lodging, and a holy rest, and peace at the last. Amen.

CHAPTER 6

Wrong about sin

In John's Gospel there is a story about a woman caught in adultery (John 8.1–11). It doesn't feature in any of the other Gospels and there is considerable doubt that this story was in the earliest manuscripts of John's Gospel. Nearly all biblical scholars think it is a later addition to the rest of the text, yet it has become one of the best known and most loved stories for probably the same reasons it was added to the Gospel. It summarizes Jesus' teaching about forgiveness, with enormous sympathy for the person who has been caught out. The onlooker hears Christ saying, 'Let anyone among you who is without sin be the first to throw a stone at her', to which John adds, 'They went away one by one, beginning with the elders.' It is kind and compassionate about what it is to be human, and gives us the immense satisfaction of seeing Jesus put the morally self-righteous in their place.

Later in John, Jesus said to his disciples that the Holy Spirit 'would prove the world wrong about sin and righteousness and judgement' (John 16.8). That the world is wrong about sin is such a strong theme in the teaching of Jesus and it should cause Christians to think long and hard before speaking about matters of morality.

What good deed must I do?

Matthew's Gospel came from a community of Jewish Christians, so it's not surprising that for Matthew the keeping of the commandments is a foundational part of the message of Jesus. Yet what is said is definitely not as expected. In chapter 19 verses 16–26, Matthew tells a crucial story for our understanding of Christian ethics: 'Someone came to Jesus and said, "Teacher, what good deed must I do to have eternal life?"' We are so used to thinking of Christianity as being about morality and doing good that we're likely to miss the point of Jesus' extraordinary answer: '"Why do you ask me about what is good? There is only one who is good."' Meaning, God alone is good. What follows is one of the most uncomfortable and important passages in the Bible.

'I have kept all the commandments,' said the rich young man, who clearly didn't feel as though he had yet entered the kingdom of heaven. There was something missing. 'What do I still lack?' So Jesus told him to do what, in effect, broke him:

> 'If you wish to be perfect, go, sell your possessions, and give the money to the poor, and you will have treasure in heaven; then come, follow me.' When the young man heard this word, he went away grieving, for he had many possessions.

Matthew knew the importance of keeping the commandments. The Sermon on the Mount, unique to his Gospel, fulfils the law given to Moses on Mount Sinai. Within it Jesus says, 'I have come not to abolish the law but to fulfil it . . . not one letter, not one stroke of a letter, will pass from the law until it is accomplished' (Matthew 5.17–18).

Matthew also knew that we long to be perfect, as our heavenly Father is perfect, and he knew our sense that we all fall short. Just before the story of the rich young man there has been a debate about marriage and divorce. Jesus' teaching is so rigorous that his disciples, not the Pharisees who had started the discussion, were astounded. This teaching is so strict and such a risk that they couldn't see anyone living up to it and said, 'it would be better not to marry'.

At the end of the story of the rich young man, Jesus said that it would be easier for a camel to pass through the eye of a needle than for a rich man to enter the kingdom of heaven. Again, *the disciples* were astounded: 'Then who can be saved?' 'Jesus looked at them and said, "For mortals [not just *rich* mortals] it is impossible, but for God all things are possible."'

What we are being told is that it is not how well we behave that is going to get us into the kingdom of heaven. That is deeply disturbing because it threatens the moral order, as indeed Jesus illustrates in the passages on either side of this story: the kingdom of heaven belongs to the likes of little children, and 'many who are first will be last, and the last will be first'. In the presence of God, there is nothing we can do to make ourselves look good. We enter the kingdom of heaven not by our own efforts, one alone is good, but because for God all things are possible. God gives us eternal life. What transforms the world and brings us into the kingdom of heaven is not our virtue but God's love.

This does not mean that what we do doesn't matter, only that any good we do is to God's glory rather than ours, and that matters a very great deal. It makes worship our prime purpose, not morality. Kenneth Kirk, in a magisterial book on moral theology, *The Vision of God*,[1] summarized the matter perfectly: 'It is not that conduct is the end of life and worship helps it, but that worship is the end of life and conduct tests it.' In worship we are ascribing ultimate and eternal worth to God. In that relationship, in which we are created, loved, judged and forgiven, we most truly know ourselves. To truly know ourselves as beloved by God is at the heart of Christianity.

Who is my neighbour?

Jesus was an observant Jew. His summary of Jewish law was 'to love God and love your neighbour as yourself'. This teaching wasn't unique, but its simplicity is distinctive and extraordinarily rigorous. Luke says that a lawyer stood up to test Jesus. He wanted to know what he must do to inherit eternal life. Jesus asked him what is written in the law. The lawyer gave the summary that in Mark and Matthew is ascribed to Jesus himself: 'You shall love the Lord your God with all your heart, and with all your soul, and with all your strength, and with all your mind; and your neighbour as yourself.' Jesus said to him, 'You have given the right answer; do this, and you will live.'

But there was a problem. Wanting to justify himself – and that is the problem – the lawyer asked Jesus, 'And who is my neighbour?' To answer, Jesus told the story of the good Samaritan (Luke 10.30–37). It is deeply shocking.

'A man was going down from Jerusalem to Jericho, and fell into the hands of robbers, who stripped him, beat him, and went away, leaving him half dead. Now by chance a priest was going down that road; and when he saw him, he passed by on the other side. So likewise a Levite, when he came to the place and saw him, passed by on the other side. But a Samaritan while travelling came near him; and when he saw him, he was moved with pity. He went to him and bandaged his wounds, having poured oil and wine on them. Then he put him on his own animal, brought him to an inn, and took care of him. The next day he took out two denarii, gave them to the innkeeper, and said, "Take care of him; and when I come back, I will repay you whatever more you spend." Which of these three, do you think, was a neighbour to the man who fell into the hands of the robbers?' He said, 'The one who showed him mercy.' Jesus said to him, 'Go and do likewise.'

The priest and the Levite were going up to Jerusalem. Had they touched a dead body they would, according to the law, have been unable to do their religious duty. It was for good reason that they passed by on the other side. Jews had no dealings with Samaritans, and the possibility of there being a *good* Samaritan was inconceivable. Yet not only did this Samaritan tend to the man who had been beaten up, he showed the lawyer what it was to be a neighbour and fulfil the law. Jesus was making a very simple point: the outsider can show the religiously observant the right way.

Who is included?

In the Acts of the Apostles chapter 8, there is a story about the baptism of an Ethiopian eunuch. It sounds exotic to us and its meaning is no longer obvious but it is one of the great missionary stories of the New Testament. Acts is volume 2 of Luke's Gospel. There is a geographical movement in Luke as Jesus goes from Galilee to Jerusalem, the geographical centre of the world and the historical centre of time. The crucifixion and resurrection are the fulcrum on which our salvation turns. Then the Acts of the Apostles has the journey going outwards from Jerusalem to the rest of the inhabited world, ending in Rome.

In the earlier part of chapter 8, Philip, and then Peter and John, proclaimed the Messiah in Samaria, north of Jerusalem. Then, 'An angel of the Lord said to Philip, "Get up and *go towards the south* to the road that goes down from Jerusalem to Gaza." (This is a wilderness road.)' What we are about to hear is desert experience: 'Now there was an Ethiopian eunuch, a court official of the Candace, queen of the Ethiopians, in charge of her entire treasury'. The gospel is going south, outwards from the Jewish world to Gentiles, and the Ethiopian is an African, a black man, from the edge of the known world.

But what is the significance of the eunuch? In Greek, the word 'eunuch' means 'the keeper of the bed chamber'. In other words he is a safe, and in himself powerless, male. Such people could be trusted to look after other people's privacy, or power, or wealth, as with the queen of Ethiopia's treasury. Throughout Mesopotamia eunuchs were given sensitive personal and political roles. But in Israel, eunuchs were despised and were outcasts. Deuteronomy 23.1 could not be a more graphic piece of legislation, making it clear that eunuchs shall not be admitted to the assembly of the Lord: 'No one whose testicles are crushed or whose penis is cut off shall be admitted to the assembly of the LORD'.

Now this eunuch was riding in his chariot down the desert road reading part of Isaiah, chapter 53. These are some of those extraordinary verses about the suffering servant that the early Church used so unexpectedly to identify Jesus as that sort of Messiah.

> Like a sheep he was led to the slaughter,
>   and like a lamb silent before its shearer,
>   so he does not open his mouth.
> In his humiliation justice was denied him.
>   Who can describe his generation?
>   For his life is taken away from the earth.

And if we read on, Isaiah 56 promises that after the restoration of Israel, the faithful eunuchs and foreigners will be gathered to the house of the Lord. The outcast will be gathered in.

Philip climbed up into the chariot and, starting with the scripture, proclaimed the good news about Jesus. When they saw water, *on the wilderness road*, the Ethiopian eunuch stopped the chariot and was baptized. Oddly, the Spirit is not linked with the baptism other than with spiriting Philip away to Caesarea to continue proclaiming the good news of Jesus Christ, leaving the poor Ethiopian eunuch to work out the implications on the rest of his life's journey and we never hear of him again.

The Church and moral issues

Why the Church falls apart over the latest moral controversy is a puzzle. Perhaps we should be less anxious because controversy often makes for some of the most creative and engaged debate about the meaning of faith, very like the rabbinic disputes of Judaism. There have always been issues, and there always will be. In the New Testament, Christians were strongly divided over whether Gentile men had to be circumcised, like Jews, in order to be Christians, and whether it was permissible to eat food that had been sacrificed to idols. Neither is top priority for us now.

Top of our list of what causes us anxiety, at least if measured by length of time given in the formal discussions of synods and international meetings, is the changing pattern of human relationships, and particularly the increasingly common sexual expression given to relationships between people of the same sex. There has to be a question about whether this is out of all proportion. From God's viewpoint surely the gap between richest and poorest, global poverty and the scandalous inequality of life expectancy in our world, and the concerns over climate change, look more important. In response to recent discussions, it is easy to imagine Jesus rising among the archbishops of the Anglican communion and saying they are straining at gnats and forgetting the weightier matters of the law to do justice, love mercy and walk humbly with God.

Frank Chikane, a pastor who was Desmond Tutu's successor as General Secretary of the South African Council of Churches, asserted that black South Africans had to reclaim the Bible, and coined the slogan 'Re-read the Bible and reinterpret it in the light of truth, and turn it against the oppressor'.[2] It is striking that Desmond Tutu, who struggled with the injustices of apartheid, sees this matter of same-sex relationships as primarily one of justice. He has said that he is ashamed of the Anglican communion on this matter.

Most of the attention given to current disputes has been given to our use of the Bible. A very curious phrase asserting 'the supreme authority of scripture' has entered the debate. It runs counter to Anglican teaching. The Church of England's Thirty-Nine Articles of Religion state that 'Holy Scripture contains all things necessary for salvation' but stops a long way short of declaring their supreme authority. For Christians, God the Father, Son and Holy Spirit, is the ultimate and supreme authority. The scriptures are one of the ways in which we are brought to God, and God is revealed to us – but they are not God. To refer to the scriptures as 'the supreme authority' seems to me a blasphemy.

Nevertheless, the problem of same-sex relationships has been presented as one in which the Bible has a plain meaning hostile to anything other than sex being confined to monogamous and lifelong marriage. Again, there is a problem of proportion, highlighted in a popular collection of quotations: 'The Bible contains 6 admonitions to homosexuals and 362 admonitions to heterosexuals. That doesn't mean that God doesn't love heterosexuals. It's just that they need more supervision.'[3]

There is also the more significant difficulty that the meaning of all six biblical passages cited in relation to homosexuality is hotly contested. Indeed, there is a case to be made that the idea of faithful, loving, same-sex relationships would have been unknown in biblical times, and no text really addresses the issue. So it is just as well that for Anglicans, Christian ethics have never simply been biblical ethics. Moral issues are decided with the use of three authorities interplaying with each other: the Bible, with its variety of literary forms and which often does not have a plain meaning; the tradition of Church teaching, a faithful wisdom from the Church down the ages; and our God-given reason and intellect. These three authorities work *together* to help us discern the work and will of God.

Human nature

In September 2006, the Anglican archbishops who identify themselves as leaders of what they call 'The Global South' issued a letter from their meeting at Kigali in Rwanda. They said they had begun their meeting at a memorial to the victims of genocide in Rwanda ten years earlier. These leaders said they

> were chastened by this experience and commit ourselves not to abandon the poor or the persecuted wherever they may be and in whatever circumstances. We add our voices to theirs and we say, 'Never again!' . . . As we prayed and wept at the mass grave of 250,000 helpless victims we confronted the utter depravity and inhumanity to which we are all subject outside of the transforming grace of God.

This is moving and sounds laudable but fails utterly to acknowledge that some Christians were directly involved in the genocide and others were complicit. The leaders of the Global South saw sin as external to themselves and in so doing they failed to take sin seriously. Theirs was a deficient, and non-scriptural, account of what it is to be human. Only if wickedness stood outside the Church and outside themselves could they then go on to imagine that the Church should exclude other people on the grounds of them being morally imperfect. The reality is that we are all morally imperfect. 'One alone is good.'

The way we understand human nature is even more significant than the use of the Bible in the divisions that have emerged among Anglicans. We have grown used to hearing, as if a legitimate expression of Christian proclamation, that one person or another is not welcome in this community of the resurrection because of some perceived moral error or flaw in their make-up. This is a very far cry from the way of Jesus, who taught that one alone is good, that a despised Samaritan can show the faithful religious how to be a good neighbour, and that even an outcast eunuch can be included in the community of the resurrection. A similar pattern is found among the disciples: impetuous Peter, who repeatedly was a bit of a let-down; and James and John, who were known as 'the sons of thunder', which suggests they had a remarkably short fuse, and who were also an embarrassment for seeking a place above the other disciples in the kingdom of heaven only to be told that the key was not personal ambition but to be a servant of others. They joined dishonest Matthew, and doubting Thomas . . . and last, and by his own admission the least of all, persecutor Paul. This motley crew are an enormous encouragement. What makes the community of the resurrection is not the disciples' moral perfection, but Easter and their willingness to be part of it, to be forgiven and accepted by God's love, to start again and have another go.

In 1979 I was ordained in St Paul's Cathedral. Each year I return with the other London clergy to renew our ordination vows. This always happens on Maundy Thursday when we remember Jesus with his disciples at the Last Supper. It's an occasion with all the complexity of Judas' betrayal, Peter's denial and the disciples' running away, leading into the desolation of Good Friday and the emptiness of Holy Saturday before the fulfilment of Easter Day. Each year I come back having failed to live up to my calling. Yet always, like the disciples back in Galilee after Easter, I am invited to be renewed, to have another go, and to break bread and drink wine in the company of Jesus, 'in memory of him'.

One of the favourite prayers used at St Martin-in-the-Fields is by the late Austen Williams. Austen himself said it is unusable now because it is in the masculine gender, but it always gets a response from congregations because it captures something accurately about what it is to be human:

I am two men;
and one is longing to serve thee utterly, and one is afraid.
O Lord have compassion upon me.

I am two men;
and one will labour to the end, and one is already weary.
O Lord have compassion upon me.

I am two men;
and one knows the suffering of the world, and one knows
    only his own.
O Lord have compassion upon me.

And may the Spirit of our Lord Jesus Christ
fill my heart and the hearts of all men everywhere.

There is a 'Sacristy Prayer' attributed to Martin Luther which
is so utterly realistic about who we clergy are and gets exactly
right our dependence on God:

Lord God, you have appointed me as a Pastor in your
Church, but you see how unsuited I am to meet so great
and difficult a task. If I had lacked your help, I would have
ruined everything long ago. Therefore, I call upon you . . .
Use me as your instrument, but do not forsake me, for if
ever I should be on my own, I would easily wreck it all.

Praying who we are might be exactly what is needed in order
to find ourselves more truly in relation to God and one another.

Church and sex

The Ethiopian eunuch was an outsider, and of such is the kingdom of heaven. We might not hear the strength of this biblical

challenge in our day. So let's try bringing this closer to home in a way that does undoubtedly challenge us by linking the story of the Ethiopian eunuch to church and sex.

The eunuch was trusted with other people's personal privacy because he was 'disinterested'. It's easy to see why that became a model for the Church, with celibate clergy, but it has its problems. Eunuchs created compensations for themselves, by increasing their own self-importance, by being the confidants of the powerful, or the trusted stewards who *also* exercised power. There are dangers here. In the Church, enforced celibacy is both an inadequate model of sexual relationships for lay people and, in the highly sexualized society we now live in, bound to play some clergy into trouble. While I am grateful that the battle against a celibate priesthood was won in the Church of England at the Reformation, what is now going on in the Roman Catholic Church hurts and damages us all.

The Church of England has a different set of issues to deal with, and if we are going to deal with them better we need to draw on models of what it means to be embodied and sexual people. Surely it is remarkable that our church has sought exemption from equal opportunity legislation intended to promote justice between people because we are unable to treat women or gay people equally? For example, in the Church of England women still cannot become bishops and some 7 per cent of parishes refuse to have women priests. We can encourage lay people to faithful same-sex relationships but cannot strengthen them to do so by blessing their relationships. Gay clergy are presented with an enforced celibacy or silent deceit, which cannot be the basis of an honest ministry. The eunuch was meant to be the outsider being brought into God's household, not the model for deceptive relationships within the household of God.

Growing up morally

In the late twentieth century an understanding of how we become mature moral beings was developed from the studies of childhood by Piaget. He observed that a small child learns right from wrong because a parent or other significant adult says 'No' very sternly in response to what is bad, or smiles warmly to reinforce what is good. The child learns the rules and aged about seven to nine years applies them in a very literal way. Gradually the child sees that this doesn't always produce the best results, so through late childhood and early adolescence, the young person starts to think about how to achieve good outcomes. Sometimes it seems best to adapt the rules, even abandon them, for a higher set of principles in order to achieve good ends. In maturity, adults respond to moral complexity, handle paradox and balance the keeping of rules with the desire for good outcomes when negotiating tricky moral dilemmas.

On this account, Jesus is a model moral teacher. He emphasized the spirit of the law and the ends it is intended to serve. He insisted on the responsibility of the individual not just to follow blindly but to seek justice. The Gospel writers, especially Matthew, portray the legalists as blind and inept in marked contrast to Jesus' clarity and goodness. Rabbi Lionel Blue got so fed up with the way Christians talked about the scribes and Pharisees on the basis of what Jesus said about them in the Gospels that he wrote a book called *To Heaven with Scribes and Pharisees*. He wanted Christians to understand that these were among the holy people of Judaism. They studied and kept the law. Psalm 119, which Christians also pray, begins:

> Happy are those whose way is blameless,
>   who walk in the law of the LORD.
> Happy are those who keep his decrees,
>   who seek him with their whole heart,

who also do no wrong,
>   but walk in his ways. (Psalm 119.1–3)

For Jews, keeping the commandments is the mark of keeping faith with God. Jews are united by the daily recitation of the *Shema*:

Hear O Israel: The LORD is our God, the LORD alone. You shall love the LORD your God with all your heart, and with all your soul, and with all your might. Keep these words that I am commanding you today in your heart. (Deuteronomy 6.4–6)

This common faith is not a system of doctrine, a creed, but a commandment to do your duty and be obedient to God.

Some of Jesus' fiercest disputes were with people who kept the letter of the law but not its spirit. We tend to hear these as Jesus saying that achieving good outcomes matters more than keeping rules. This suits our own contemporary desire for independence of thought and action, but that is certainly not what Jesus had in mind. He argued that doing your duty matters and that the detailed application of the commandments includes specific case law where the duty of care overrides other commandments. For example in Luke 13.10–17 his argument about the healing of a woman on the Sabbath was not to overturn the commandment to keep the Sabbath holy and free from work, but to argue the priority of laws. If you can take an animal to drink on the Sabbath, how much more important is the healing of someone who has been sick for 18 years? It was an attack on hypocrisy made in a recognizably rabbinic way, the energy of which created engaged religious observance.

Judge not

Forgiveness is at the heart of the teaching of Jesus. Jesus said that the person who has been forgiven much is the person who will love much (Luke 7.47). As God is with us, so we should be with one another. 'Forgive us our sins as we have forgiven those who sin against us' is a key phrase in the Lord's Prayer.

Jesus' teaching about forgiveness is aimed at those who were sure of their own goodness and looked down on everyone else.

> Two men went up to the temple to pray, one a Pharisee and the other a tax-gatherer. The Pharisee stood up and prayed thus: 'I thank thee, O God, that I am not like the rest of men, greedy, dishonest, adulterous; or, for that matter, like this tax-gatherer. I fast twice a week; I pay tithes on all that I get.' But the other kept his distance and would not even raise his eyes to heaven, but beat upon his breast saying, 'O God, have mercy on me, sinner that I am.' It was this man, I tell you, and not the other, who went home acquitted of his sins. For everyone who exalts himself will be humbled; and whoever humbles himself will be exalted. (Luke 18.9–14, NEB)

Look around any church and you will find a great mix of humanity. No one is perfect, but Christians have glimpsed the possibility of being called to share in the glory of God's extravagantly generous kingdom, so generous it might even include me. This does not mean that anything goes, but all are welcome and none should throw stones: 'Judge not, that ye be not judged'. This isn't false humility but the recognition that in all honesty we have much to be humble about. If we began from that premise, the discussions of the Anglican communion would be transformed. If only we had the confidence to live in Christ, there is a truth with the power to set us free.

CHAPTER 7

A Good Friday church:
six addresses on Saint John's Passion

Churches have very different characters. Some are Pentecostal and are characterized by the liveliness of the Holy Spirit. Pope John Paul II spoke of the Roman Catholic Church saying, 'We are an Easter people and Alleluia is our song.' Before I came to St Martin's I was told it is 'the Christmas church'. There certainly is a lot of Christmas at St Martin's but I have come to see its defining character as that of a Good Friday church. The three-hour service on Good Friday is the liturgical centre of St Martin's year. It reflects the accounts of the crucifixion in the Gospels of Matthew, Mark and Luke in which we are told there was darkness over the whole land from noon until three in the afternoon. St John's Passion is different and tells of the glory of the cross on which Christ was raised up. These addresses come from the three-hour service in 2007 when the church was scaffolded during the major buildings renewal. A phrase from a poem by R. S. Thomas had provided an obvious Lent theme, 'The Scaffolding of the Spirit', had provided an obvious Lent theme. The sections of St John's Gospel read at the service are printed and I have included references to the sections of Bach's *St John Passion* which were sung so that you can, if you want, listen to them and hear the interplay with the reflections on the Passion of Christ.

1. Whom are you looking for?

Reading: John 18.1–11

After Jesus had spoken these words, he went out with his disciples across the Kidron valley to a place where there was a garden, which he and his disciples entered. Now Judas, who betrayed him, also knew the place, because Jesus often met there with his disciples. So Judas brought a detachment of soldiers together with police from the chief priests and the Pharisees, and they came there with lanterns and torches and weapons. Then Jesus, knowing all that was to happen to him, came forward and asked them, 'For whom are you looking?' They answered, 'Jesus of Nazareth.' Jesus replied, 'I am he.' Judas, who betrayed him, was standing with them. When Jesus said to them, 'I am he,' they stepped back and fell to the ground. Again he asked them, 'For whom are you looking?' And they said, 'Jesus of Nazareth.' Jesus answered, 'I told you that I am he. So if you are looking for me, let these men go.' This was to fulfil the word that he had spoken, 'I did not lose a single one of those whom you gave me.' Then Simon Peter, who had a sword, drew it, struck the high priest's slave, and cut off his right ear. The slave's name was Malchus. Jesus said to Peter, 'Put your sword back into its sheath. Am I not to drink the cup that the Father has given me?'

Bach, St John Passion:
1. Lord, Thou our Master . . . for ever glorified

Written in 1724, just as the present St Martin's church building was moving towards its completion, the brooding, tense, multi-layered turbulence of that opening of Bach's *St John Passion* sets the mood perfectly for our three hours here at the cross of

Christ. Whom are you looking for, and what is his significance?

Richard Burridge, the Dean of King's College just along the Strand, says that the Gospels of Jesus are more like classical biographies than we used to think. He says an account of the way a person died reveals what they lived for. Each Gospel gives a distinctive account of how they see Jesus. The different pictures are complementary, different aspects of a complex person.

We are so used to reading all four Gospels as if they were one, that we miss just how distinctive is John's account of Jesus. There is no agony in the Garden of Gethsemane in John, no sleeping disciples contrasted with a praying Christ asking if it is possible for this cup to pass from him. John's Jesus simply says, 'Am I not to drink the cup that the father has given me?' The unfolding of the story provides its own answer in which Jesus takes his part freely, willingly.

John's Gospel gives us the grand picture. The creative Word of God, which was in the beginning, is identified with the particular being of Jesus of Nazareth. Love is made known in the humble service of a master washing his disciples' feet, in the feeding of the hungry with the bread of life, and healing the sick. God is known in the light of the world, water of life, bread of heaven, true vine . . . each of which, in Christ, is eternal.

John's contrast with those who came to arrest Jesus could not be more striking. They came by night, with lanterns, torches and weapons. They had to ask for him twice, and even though he came forward, they fell to the ground. Peter also tried to evade the moment by the use of force. It's as if Jesus is so self-possessed that he had to help them fulfil their part in this drama, and when they took him away they even bound him!

In John, Jesus knows his destiny, and accepts it willingly because he is in the Father and the Father is in him. The fact that they are one has the potential to change everything for the world. In the verses at the end of chapter 17, just before we began to read, Jesus said:

Righteous Father, the world does not know you, but I know you; and these [disciples] know that you have sent me. I made your name known to them, and I will make it known, so that the love with which you have loved me may be in them, and I in them. (John 17.25–26)

We often think of the glory of Christ as coming from the resurrection and ascension, but in John's Gospel the glory of God is seen here and now in Jesus' acceptance of the cross. In chapter 17 again, verse 1, 'Father, the hour has come; glorify your Son so that the Son may glorify you.'

In 2005 Archbishop Desmond Tutu, preaching at St Martin-in-the-Fields, used a Johannine insight memorably when he said that, 'Christ when he was raised on the cross did not say "I draw *some* people to myself." He said I draw all, All, ALL.' The Passion of Jesus is a moment of cosmic significance – God so loved *the world*, not just people like us, or the Church – and *all* who have been given into Christ's hands will be safe.

That's a far cry from the way in the modern Church where Christians of different flavours often see their view of Christ as exclusive and in competition. William Blake, one of London's visionaries, derided this long ago in 'The Everlasting Gospel':

> The Vision of Christ that thou dost see
> Is my vision's greatest enemy.
> Thine has a great hook nose like thine;
> Mine has a snub nose like to mine.
> Thine is the Friend of all Mankind;
> Mine speaks in parables to the blind.
> Thine loves the same world that mine hates;
> Thy heaven doors are my hell gates . . .
>
> And Caiaphas was in his own mind
> A benefactor to mankind.

Both read the Bible day and night,
But thou read'st black where I read white . . .

I am sure this Jesus will not do,
Either for Englishman or Jew.

'For whom are you looking?' Here is God among us; Jesus abiding in God and abiding with us, one with us. The glory of the Passion of Jesus is of God sharing what it is to be human and transforming it so that humanity becomes divine. There's glory for you.

'Whom do you seek?'; 'Jesus of Nazareth', and in a phrase intentionally laden with the presence of God, Jesus replied, 'I am.'

2. Are you one of this man's disciples?

Reading: John 18.12–27

So the soldiers, their officer, and the Jewish police arrested Jesus and bound him. First they took him to Annas, who was the father-in-law of Caiaphas, the high priest that year. Caiaphas was the one who had advised the Jews that it was better to have one person die for the people.

Simon Peter and another disciple followed Jesus. Since that disciple was known to the high priest, he went with Jesus into the courtyard of the high priest, but Peter was standing outside at the gate. So the other disciple, who was known to the high priest, went out, spoke to the woman who guarded the gate, and brought Peter in. The woman said to Peter, 'You are not also one of this man's disciples, are you?' He said, 'I am not.' Now the slaves and the police had made a charcoal fire because it was cold, and they were standing round it and warming themselves. Peter also was standing with them and warming himself.

Then the high priest questioned Jesus about his disciples and about his teaching. Jesus answered, 'I have spoken openly to the world; I have always taught in synagogues and in the temple, where all the Jews come together. I have said nothing in secret. Why do you ask me? Ask those who heard what I said to them; they know what I said.' When he had said this, one of the police standing nearby struck Jesus on the face, saying, 'Is that how you answer the high priest?' Jesus answered, 'If I have spoken wrongly, testify to the wrong. But if I have spoken rightly, why do you strike me?' Then Annas sent him bound to Caiaphas the high priest.

Now Simon Peter was standing and warming himself. They asked him, 'You are not also one of his disciples, are you?' He denied it and said, 'I am not.' One of the slaves of the high priest, a relative of the man whose ear Peter had cut off, asked, 'Did I not see you in the garden with him?' Again Peter denied it, and at that moment the cock crowed.

Bach, St John Passion: *Aria (Soprano):*
9. I follow thee also with joy to be near Thee

The text Bach set to music as the *St John Passion* was the Gospel narrative combined with poetic texts from a variety of sources. When it came to Peter's denial, Bach seems to have felt the need to increase the drama by importing the detail from Matthew and Luke that after the cock crowed, Peter went out and wept bitterly, as each of us who have tried to follow Jesus will at some time have done.

In a stroke of genius, Bach preceded Peter's denial with that sublime aria, 'I follow thee also with joy to be near Thee'. It is one of the most beautiful pieces of music in the world. It is also what I long for and aspire to spiritually: following Jesus with joy.

Each of us is complex, and though we strive for personal integration and unity, most of us have known times when we just don't 'add up'. As part of our exploration of 'the scaffolding of the spirit' this Lent, five members of the St Martin's community spoke on Sunday evenings in response to the question, 'Why am I still a Christian?' For some of our speakers there had been times of considerable struggle with life and faith. There's a pattern that the treasure was found when the going was tough. Smoothness produces smooth people, but a bit of grit can produce a pearl.

As we read the scriptures we find ourselves identifying with different characters: Peter and the other disciples, the High Priest, the soldiers, the servant girl, Mary and the other women. In the reading of the Passion that takes place in churches on Palm Sunday, there used to be a tradition that the priest took the role not of Jesus but of Judas. It was said this was so that the burden of voicing betrayal did not fall on any lay person, but as I have got older I have wondered if it is also that every priest knows the extremes of both the joy of Christ being with us *and* the burden of our own betrayals.

What happens to Judas doesn't seem to be of much interest to John. Judas did what he had to do and we hear no more of him after the betrayal and arrest of Jesus. This is at one with Jesus being in control and doing the Father's will; Judas played his part. But for those of us who also know about betrayal, the problem of Judas is fascinating.

Judas must have thought there was no way back in to fellowship with Christ. What he did was so terrible that it cut him off for ever, whereas Peter allowed Jesus to get the relationship going again. In John chapter 21, that curious restorative 'add on' after the formal end of the Gospel, the risen Lord appeared to the disciples who had gone back to the Sea of Galilee. In asking Simon Peter three times, 'Simon, son of John, do you love me?' and Peter affirming, 'Yes Lord, you know I love you', 'Feed my sheep', it's as though Peter is being restored by cancelling out his denial. Jesus then points to Peter's own death in Rome for having followed Christ faithfully.

Talking about the many people who come to the monastery on retreat, the Abbot of Worth said that people sometimes come in order to discern what is right for them; but of course the other aspect is that having discerned, they must *obey* what it is they have discerned. That is a lot more difficult, as every preacher knows.

Sometimes at Communion we use an invitation from the Iona community:

> Come to this table
> You who have much faith and you who would like to have
>   more;
> You who have been to this sacrament often and you who
>   have not been for a long time;
> You who have tried to follow Jesus and you who have
>   failed.
> Come. It is Christ who invites us to meet him here.

And you? 'Are you not also one of this man's disciples?'

3. So, you are a King

Reading: John 18.28–40

Then they took Jesus from Caiaphas to Pilate's headquarters. It was early in the morning. They themselves did not enter the headquarters, so as to avoid ritual defilement and to be able to eat the Passover. So Pilate went out to them and said, 'What accusation do you bring against this man?' They answered, 'If this man were not a criminal, we would not have handed him over to you.' Pilate said to them,

'Take him yourselves and judge him according to your law.'
The Jews replied, 'We are not permitted to put anyone to
death.' (This was to fulfil what Jesus had said when he indi-
cated the kind of death he was to die.)

Then Pilate entered the headquarters again, summoned
Jesus, and asked him, 'Are you the King of the Jews?' Jesus
answered, 'Do you ask this on your own, or did others tell
you about me?' Pilate replied, 'I am not a Jew, am I? Your
own nation and the chief priests have handed you over to
me. What have you done?' Jesus answered, 'My kingdom is
not from this world. If my kingdom were from this world,
my followers would be fighting to keep me from being
handed over to the Jews. But as it is, my kingdom is not
from here.' Pilate asked him, 'So you are a king?' Jesus
answered, 'You say that I am a king. For this I was born,
and for this I came into the world, to testify to the truth.
Everyone who belongs to the truth listens to my voice.'
Pilate asked him, 'What is truth?'

After he had said this, he went out to the Jews again and
told them, 'I find no case against him. But you have a
custom that I release someone for you at the Passover. Do
you want me to release for you the King of the Jews?' They
shouted in reply, 'Not this man, but Barabbas!' Now
Barabbas was a bandit.

Bach, St John Passion: *23 a–g*

Evangelist:	But the Jews cried out and shouted to Pilate . . .
Chorus:	If thou let this man go, thou art no friend of Caesar's . . .
Evangelist:	Then when Pilate heard them speaking thus . . .
Chorus:	Away with him, away with him.
Evangelist:	Pilate saith unto them . . .

Chorus: We have no King but Caesar.
Evangelist: And then he delivered him to them that they might crucify him.

'Is it lawful to pay taxes to Caesar?' was a trick question intended to catch Jesus out. He took a coin and asked them whose image was on it. 'Render to Caesar the things that are Caesar's but to God the things that are God's.' That enigmatic answer gave rise to 2,000 years of debate about whether and how the followers of Christ should be involved in politics. In the second century, Tertullian suggested a different and, for Jews, more obvious understanding. 'And you, whose image is on you? Render to God the things that are God's.' Hear it that way and it's harder to split the personal from the political, the things of Caesar's from the things of God.

Religious leaders don't come out well in any of the Gospels, but neither here before Pilate does the religious group. They kept themselves outside Pilate's headquarters so as to remain pure for the Passover, while shouting for the death of an innocent man. Our capacity for self-deception can be pretty big, but groups behave differently to individuals and can take on a sort of animus that no individual would own.

One of the most influential theologians of the twentieth century was the American Reinhold Niebuhr. His book *Moral Man, Immoral Society*[1] said that individuals could be moral in a way that groups never can. Groups are about politics and power, and people in public life need to understand that difference. We'll do and say things in groups we just wouldn't do individually. How else could a group of probably ordinary individuals shout for the release of Barabbas the bandit over an innocent man?

It is difficult for the individual to stand over against the group. Most of us don't like the sense of isolation and you have to be pretty confident in your own judgement to say that the group has got it wrong. Then something snaps and in conscience you can't do otherwise.

There's an odd culture in the Church at the moment. We are obsessed about homosexuality. Before the meeting of Anglican archbishops in February 2007, the Archbishop of Cape Town said that in Africa God might be more concerned with poverty, war, famine and AIDS than homosexuality. Here in the West End it does seem amazing that the Church has so much to say about the behaviour of a minority of people whose orientation is to same-sex relationships and so little to say about the exploitation of people through prostitution and the sex trade. In the equivalent of our 'standing outside the headquarters', we have missed the weightier matters of the religious law – of justice in the face of exploitation and of a selfish consumer culture in which promiscuous sex is a commodity to be bought for what masquerades as personal fulfilment.

According to Father Ken Leech, who recently retired after a long ministry, mostly in east London, Christianity is ambivalent about cities, with a lengthy anti-urban polemic on the one hand, and a vision of the city of God, the holy city, on the other. Yet Christianity was, in origin, an urban movement, so much so that the words 'pagan' ('people of the countryside') and 'heathen' ('people of the heath') were used in contrast to urban Christians. Ken writes,

> It is a central task of urban theology to question, undermine and expose false values which put profits before people, private gain before public good, and ultimately the success of enterprise before the welfare of the city and all its people.[2]

Bob Hope once said, 'London's a wonderful city, or at least it will be when it's finished.' The recognition that Christ is a King means that we have glimpsed the beliefs and values by which we wish to live and build ourselves, the Church and our city. Individually and together we commit ourselves to try to live in response to a personal and corporate vision of the kingdom of God, not to join in the shouting for the blood of an easy victim.

Why are we so blind to some things and so willing to go along with the crowd? Standing before Pilate, even if we are part of the religious group and have kept our purity by standing outside Pilate's headquarters, Christ questions us all.

4. The scaffolding of spirit

Reading: John 19.16b–25a

So they took Jesus; and carrying the cross by himself, he went out to what is called The Place of the Skull, which in Hebrew is called Golgotha. There they crucified him, and with him two others, one on either side, with Jesus between them. Pilate also had an inscription written and put on the cross. It read, 'Jesus of Nazareth, the King of the Jews.' Many of the Jews read this inscription, because the place where Jesus was crucified was near the city; and it was written in Hebrew, in Latin, and in Greek. Then the chief priests of the Jews said to Pilate, 'Do not write, "The King of the Jews," but, "This man said, I am King of the Jews."' Pilate answered, 'What I have written I have written.' When the soldiers had crucified Jesus, they took his clothes and divided them into four parts, one for each soldier. They also took his tunic; now the tunic was seamless, woven in one piece from the top. So they said to one another, 'Let us not tear it, but cast lots for it to see who will get it'. This was to fulfil what the scripture says,

'They divided my clothes among themselves,
and for my clothing they cast lots.'

And that is what the soldiers did.

Meanwhile, standing near the cross of Jesus were his mother, and his mother's sister, Mary the wife of Clopas, and Mary Magdalene.

Bach, St John Passion*:*

25 *Evangelist:* And there they crucified him.
    Chorus: Write him not as our King ...
    Evangelist: And Pilate answered ...
26 *Chorale:* Within my heart's recesses their sprinkles bright.

The music of that chorale has become for us the tune for the Palm Sunday processional hymn, 'All glory, laud and honour, to thee redeemer king'. We will use it again as we process out at the end of the service, the kingship of Christ having been revealed in the course of Holy Week by the stark events of the crucifixion. What is revealed is God, truth, love, things that are eternal; and the soldiers divided his clothes by casting lots. In a haunting phrase, T. S. Eliot speaks of our having the experience but missing the meaning.

This Lent, I have loved our using the R. S. Thomas poem, 'Emerging':

> ... *it is matter* is the scaffolding
> of spirit ...

Matter limits and restricts us. That's why dualism is so attractive. If only we could be free of these earthly bonds, we would have limitless possibility and be free spirits. But matter, which restricts, limits and confines, is also what provides the scaffold, or framework, that makes any creativity possible.

Like Michelangelo's sculpture in stone, the words of Thomas' poem continue:

as form in sculpture is the prisoner
of the hard rock, so in everyday life
it is the plain facts and natural happenings
that conceal God and reveal him to us
little by little under the mind's tooling.

Of course, matter is ambiguous and can be used for good and evil. In fundraising for our present building work, and only very occasionally and under the pressure that the bills have to be paid, I have found myself remembering General Booth, the founder of the Salvation Army, who said, 'Give me your filthy money and I will make it clean'. But actually, what we are able to do is made possible by the economy of the city and world in which we are set.

It was with quite a shock when reading a book about the abolition of slavery that I realized a significant part of London's wealth in the eighteenth century came from the slave trade. This church, built between 1721 and 1726, must have benefited indirectly from a trade that killed between 9 million and 15 million. We're tainted, not, I hope, irredeemably, because we exist in creation, in a material world.

When I taught at a theological college, training clergy, a new student told me that coming to college was like eating the apple. All his innocence about Church had disappeared and there was no going back. I should think there will be those on the council of this church, or on the Church of England's Pensions Board, who would recognize that observation. According to Monsignor Ronnie Knox, writing I think in the 1950s, 'He who is prone to sea sickness should not go down into the engine room of the barque of Rome!'

At the time of his writing the *St John Passion*, Bach was a church musician. It is sobering to discover that in April 1723 he was the *third* choice for the post of Kantor at St Thomas' Church in Leipzig behind Telemann, whom most of us will have heard of, and Graupner, whom most of us will not; both of whom for very different reasons turned the job down.

Bach must have had something to prove. In five years he wrote 150 cantatas, as well as the *Magnificat* (1723) and the *St John* (1724) and *St Matthew Passions* (1727). He had finite musical resources available to him: 16 first-choir singers and up to 18 instrumentalists. Cantatas were performed at 7.30 in the morning. *The Oxford Companion to Music* comments, 'It is not unlikely that some of the performances were poor'. In 1730, increasingly disenchanted with the conditions at St Thomas' Church, Bach submitted a memorandum to the church authorities setting out his minimum requirements for well-regulated church music. Their response was to threaten to reduce his salary.

Every musician, artist or architect needs a patron. You can't be an artist in theory or abstract. Art requires commitment in particular material. Yet, Christ's crucifixion makes clear that our lives are not defined by how well life goes, or by our good or bad luck. There are people who live transfigured in outwardly unpromising circumstances. I am often struck how people visiting a friend or relative in a hospice come away saying, 'If only we could live like that all the time.' It's as if, being near to death, we know how precious love is and how it transcends the moment.

Standing near the cross of Christ, in the less than promising place called Golgotha, God is revealed to us in such a way that within the limits of our lives we are offered the opportunity to be fully human.

5. The vision of God

Reading: John 19.25–30

And that is what the soldiers did. Meanwhile, standing near the cross of Jesus were his mother, and his mother's sister,

Mary the wife of Clopas, and Mary Magdalene. When Jesus saw his mother and the disciple whom he loved standing beside her, he said to his mother, 'Woman, here is your son.' Then he said to the disciple, 'Here is your mother.' And from that hour the disciple took her into his own home.

After this, when Jesus knew that all was now finished, he said (in order to fulfil the scripture), 'I am thirsty.' A jar full of sour wine was standing there. So they put a sponge full of the wine on a branch of hyssop and held it to his mouth. When Jesus had received the wine, he said, 'It is finished.' Then he bowed his head and gave up his spirit.

Bach, St John Passion*: Aria (bass) and chorus:*
32. O thou my Saviour give me answer

Then he bowed his head and gave up his spirit.

It is curiously difficult for us, so familiar with Matthew, Mark and Luke, to get tuned to what John is saying about Jesus. His account of the crucifixion is shorter than the other evangelists'. The time between crucifixion and death is briefer than in Mark, and in Mark it was so brief that Pilate was amazed. In Mark the crucifixion was at 9 a.m. and the death of Jesus at 3 p.m. In John he was still before Pilate at midday and died in time to be buried before evening.

In John, there was no Simon of Cyrene: Jesus carried his own cross. There was no mocking, no darkness, no centurion, no cry of dereliction. He was not 'done to' but in control, knowing what would happen and willing it to be accomplished. No one took his life from him. Of his own accord, he gave up his spirit, laying down his life in obedience to the Father. Jesus gave his life out of love for his friends. He did it that we might have abundant life and he did it majestically.

At the end of chapter 20 John concludes that he has written, 'so that you may come to believe that Jesus is the Messiah, the Son of God, and that through believing you may have life in his name'.

For those who agree with Richard Dawkins, all religion is bad religion. Certainly there is plenty of evidence for him to draw on, but we could counter by suggesting that there is also bad science and harmful applications of science without needing to suggest that all science is bad. What good religion does is to draw us in to the worship of God, and John's point is that in truth, good religion is life giving.

In this there is a very definite account of being human and living fully. The essence of Christianity is that our greatest happiness is to be found 'in' God. In John's Gospel Jesus says, 'I am in the Father and the Father is in me.' Being 'in' implies being one, and this is done so that we may be drawn in and also be at one, indwelling in God.

At the Maundy Thursday Eucharist, I was struck again how Jesus gives us a lesson in loving service. The master washes his disciples' feet, and we are called to wash one another's feet. In our culture, this is not the most popular management model or strategy for self-improvement. What Jesus is offering is a model of selflessness in which, having the confidence to lose ourselves in love, we will find ourselves in God.

The Christian calling is to unselfishness and that sort of personal disinterestedness associated with, say, a judge hearing a case and determining judgement without thought of personal gain. What matters is the truth, and we stand under it.

In one of my favourite books of Christian theology, *The Vision of God*,[3] Kenneth Kirk wrote that the way in which unselfishness is attained is through worship. 'Worship lifts the soul out of its preoccupation with itself and its activities, and centres its aspirations entirely on God.' He warns us 'not to confuse worship with the quest for "religious experience" (so very popular in our day) nor with the employment of devout thoughts to stimulate moral effort (much less popular), for both these counterfeits to worship lend themselves only too readily to egocentricism'. Worship 'disinfects our egoism'. It is 'something which *comes upon* the soul, not which is achieved by it'.

In John's Gospel, the key to Jesus' selfless love is his being obedient and 'in' or at one with God – fully divine *and* fully human. Raised up on the cross we see his glory, and in worship we find ourselves raised up with him.

6. The day of preparation

Reading: John 19.31–42

> Since it was the day of Preparation, the Jews did not want the bodies left on the cross during the sabbath, especially because that sabbath was a day of great solemnity. So they asked Pilate to have the legs of the crucified men broken and the bodies removed. Then the soldiers came and broke the legs of the first and of the other who had been crucified with him. But when they came to Jesus and saw that he was already dead, they did not break his legs. Instead, one of the soldiers pierced his side with a spear, and at once blood and water came out. (He who saw this has testified so that you also may believe. His testimony is true, and he knows that he tells the truth.) These things occurred so that the scripture might be fulfilled, 'None of his bones shall be broken.' And again another passage of scripture says, 'They will look on the one whom they have pierced.'
>
> After these things, Joseph of Arimathea, who was a disciple of Jesus, though a secret one because of his fear of the Jews, asked Pilate to let him take away the body of Jesus. Pilate gave him permission; so he came and removed his body. Nicodemus, who had at first come to Jesus by night, also came, bringing a mixture of myrrh and aloes, weighing

about a hundred pounds. They took the body of Jesus and wrapped it with the spices in linen cloths, according to the burial custom of the Jews. Now there was a garden in the place where he was crucified, and in the garden there was a new tomb in which no one had ever been laid. And so, because it was the Jewish day of Preparation, and the tomb was nearby, they laid Jesus there.

Bach, St John Passion: *39. Chorus, Rest well*

Unlike the other Gospels, John says that the crucifixion took place on 'the day of Preparation'. There was urgency to get the bodies down from the cross so that the Jews would be ready for the Passover Festival. So they asked Pilate to have the legs of the crucified men broken to hasten their deaths. Again, what is revealed is that Jesus has already given up his life freely, and that in keeping with scripture and the will of God, not one bone has been broken. The soldier pierces his side and what flows out are water and blood, symbols of life – the water of life, baptism, new birth; the blood of the new covenant which we drink in the Eucharist to share in the resurrection.

Joseph of Arimathea, a secret disciple, and Nicodemus, who came to Jesus by night, are the people who take charge of his burial. The words, 'The Jews', get repeated and emphasized as though this day of preparation is the one that will reveal what John the Baptist declared at the beginning of the Gospel: 'Look, here is the lamb of God.' This is a burial and a day of preparation showing the glory of God. This Passover lamb will bring a new freedom tonight, and tomorrow Joseph and Nicodemus will no longer need to be secret followers of Christ. They will come to him in daylight. This day of preparation is bursting with the latent energy of new life.

On 28 March 2003, 19-year-old Trooper Chris Finney was

driving one of two armoured vehicles north of Basrah in Iraq when they came under what is euphemistically called 'friendly fire'. Finney got himself out of the burning vehicle but saw that his gunner was trapped. At no small risk to himself, he went back into the blazing vehicle, munitions exploding around him, and pulled the gunner free and to relative safety. Wounded himself, he went back to the vehicle and sent a message to head-quarters identifying their position and stating what had happened. As the American planes lined up to come in a second time, he realized that another soldier was trapped in the other vehicle. He tried to get him out but this time failed, collapsing at the side of the blazing vehicles. He was awarded the George Cross (not the Victoria Cross because this was not in enemy action) with a citation that concluded:

> During these attacks and their horrifying aftermath, Trooper Finney displayed clear-headed courage and devotion to his comrades which was out of all proportion to his age and experience. Acting with complete disregard for his own safety even when wounded, his bravery was of the highest order throughout.

Because the vicar of St Martin's is chaplain to the Victoria Cross and George Cross Association, I was able to ask Chris Finney what made him do it. He replied, 'It's what you do for your mates. It was instinct, anyone would have done it.'

Lots of people have tried to analyse what it is that prepares people to behave like this under pressure in the moment they are tested. There is no formula. Being well trained and establishing good habits certainly helps. I have heard a surgeon talk about the way in which he fell back on instincts formed in his training when an operation went wrong and he didn't have time to think out what to do. We probably all have some examples from our own lives when we have just scrambled through until we have the time to stop and reflect.

St Martin's went through a period of preparation, more like two years than a day, and the planning before that was extensive and arduous. Between the first Sunday of May and the last Sunday of September 2007 the church was closed and we were 'St Martin's on Tour' working regularly on nine different sites. Our one absolute commitment to remain here was the temporary building for the most vulnerable and needy who turn to us for help through The Connection at St Martin's.

The presence of The Connection, which sees 6,000 homeless people a year, ensures we are an earthly sort of church. Perhaps it is one of the reasons we are so evidently a Good Friday church, with this three-hour service the liturgical centrepiece of our annual cycle of worship. In this community, people who know their own complex vulnerability gather around the cross of Jesus and we find ourselves transformed by God's love. In John's account of the Passion of Christ, the day of preparation already bears much fruit. We now wait for the risen lamb of God, and our being brought to a new freedom in the community of the resurrection on Easter Day.

CHAPTER 8

A sermon for Easter Day

Good Friday is the one day in the year when I do not hang around after the service. I can't. It may be *Good* Friday but by the end of that service I am *good* for nothing, and only want to flee the company of others. There is good precedent. Most of the disciples fled when Jesus was arrested. They didn't even stay for the crucifixion. At most, Mary, John and some other of the women stayed with Jesus to the end. John has them intimately present: 'There at the foot of the cross stood Mary his mother'. Matthew and Mark say the women looked on from a distance. Luke adds 'all his acquaintances' to the women watching at a distance, probably out of embarrassment that the disciples were said by Mark and Matthew to have fled as soon as the trouble began.

The events remembered in Holy Week dislocate us as human beings and as a community of the followers of Jesus. The way in which the crowd turned from welcoming Jesus as King on Palm Sunday, to shouting for him to be crucified on Good Friday, is a salutary reminder of the power and infidelity of the mob. As I have got older I have also come to see that what happens to Judas and Peter is one of the turning points of the story and illustrates our salvation with painful clarity.

Both Peter and Judas were among the Twelve for the Last Supper. When it came to the foot-washing Peter thought it all quite wrong until Jesus explained. Then Peter exclaimed, 'Lord, not my feet only but also my hands and my head!' (John 13.9). Jesus washed Judas' feet as well as the others'.

Why Judas betrayed Jesus is one of the great puzzles. It's unlikely he was acting out of selfish greed, betraying his Lord for 30 pieces of silver – more likely that he felt let down that Jesus hadn't delivered the freedom he had promised. '"The one I kiss is the man; arrest him". At once he came to Jesus and said, "Greetings, Rabbi!" and he kissed him' (Matthew 26.49).

Peter also fell into the trap. 'Before the cock crows you will deny me three times'. He followed to see what was going on. It was only a servant girl who asked him if he was one of the men with Jesus. It wasn't like a police interrogator or anyone significant. He wanted to stay close by, to see what was going on. It didn't matter that he said he didn't even know the man, until the cock crowed.

Putting ourselves outside the company of Jesus, putting ourselves into exile, is common human experience. But for neither Judas nor Peter does the issue turn on what they did or their motives for doing it. It turns on their response to having done something unimaginably dreadful. Judas went out and hanged himself in despair that such treachery could never be put right. Peter went out and wept bitterly, but for him it was not all over.

What in some ways is an odd addition to John's Gospel, chapter 21, is one of my favourite passages in scripture. It is about the way in which, in the resurrection, Christ builds again the new community of disciples. Three times he asked, 'Peter, do you love me?' and Peter answered three times in a way that seems intended to cancel his denials, 'Yes, Lord, you know I love you'. Christ does this with each one of us in the Eucharist on Easter morning. It is the way in which the community of those who would be followers of Jesus is put back together again in the resurrection. What we are faced with is recognizably the same in ourselves and in each other and somehow completely different because of the way Christ meets us anew. So, here are three things that make this Easter community distinctive.

First, we have learnt from our own experience that it will be good for us to be generous about the shortcomings of others. It's enlightened self-interest, of course, that they *might* then be generous to us. I was struck by the Response in the Good Friday liturgy in which we said, 'Not because he was perfect, *but because he refused to be divided,* He was crucified, dead and buried.' He refused to be divided from his true nature, refused to give in to the all-too-plausible temptations that would have split him and divided his very being in such a way as to make him impotent and therefore no threat to anyone. But we – although in truth I can only speak for myself – *have* experienced being divided, 'through negligence, weakness, our own deliberate fault'. Even then, what is asked of us is to be open to the possibility of encountering the risen Christ and allowing him to remake us and our community. This resurrection is of people who know about forgiveness. In the teaching of Jesus it is the person who has been forgiven much who knows how to love much. The Church, the worldwide Anglican communion, seems to be slow to get this fact about ourselves.

Second, truth took a battering in Holy Week. Pilate's sigh, 'What is truth?', reminds us that truth-telling can be a politically expedient exercise. When politicians say, 'The fact is . . .' you know that what follows will probably be a value-driven assertion. Philosophically, 'Truth' is tricky. I don't much like the word 'integrity' either. When applied to Christians and our churches it too easily implies self-righteousness and self-satisfaction. In the Anglican communion, 'We have integrity' seems to suggest that 'they' might not. 'Integrity' is not commonly understood to mean those who know their need of God.

But I have been helped to see that in the resurrection community it is *honesty* that Christians should be concerned with. It is simpler than truth and integrity – more of a process, a striving rather than an absolute. The community that fled and has now been regrouped around the risen Lord is called to be straightforward, to tell it as it is, to be honest in our dealings with each other and the world. No longer do we need to come to Jesus by night, nor the darkness in the middle of the day as on Good Friday when Truth was crucified. Walking in the light, as honestly as we can, is the only basis on which we can make trusting relationships, and without trust the whole social structure falls apart through fear and suspicion. So attempting to be honest is as distinctive a mark as forgiveness for the resurrection community.

Third, the fact of our own sinfulness and of the potential for wickedness within our world, so realistically held before us in the Passion of Christ, should have the effect of shaking our complacency. I am very taken by a phrase used by Canon Andrew Shanks of Manchester Cathedral when he speaks of 'the solidarity of the shaken'. He gained this phrase from the Czech philosopher Jan Patocka. In 1977, Patocka founded Charter 77 as a group campaigning for basic human rights that were, in theory, protected by law but in practice were not protected at all. So Patocka, an elderly man, was arrested, beaten up by the security police, and died of his injuries. Andrew Shanks says that not long before he died, Patocka published, or hadn't published because in fact he couldn't publish in his own country, but had issued through samizdat (self-publishing), an essay in which he wrote about the First World War and the solidarity that never emerged between people on both sides, Germans and the Allies, who had been shaken by their experience of war. He suggested that if peace were to have been truly experienced, it would have required solidarity on the basis of their common shakenness.

You can see the solidarity of the shaken in the way the community of disciples was re-established on the basis of fleeting encounters with the risen Lord. You can sense it in our own experience as we realize that nothing can separate us from the love of God in Christ Jesus. The solidarity of the shaken will be generous, open, forgiving, looking forward not back. Those who have ever glimpsed the kingdom of God cannot be content with the world where there is so much war and so little fairness.

In the resurrection, we are a community of the shaken. We long for God's kingdom to come on earth as it is in heaven.

Forgiveness, honesty and the 'solidarity of the shaken' are three of the marks of the community of the resurrection. Is it a good way? In the light of the shared experience with Christ we rehearse at Easter, I believe it is the only way.

CHAPTER 9

The renewal of St Martin's

As with most things, the idea of a £36 million renewal of St Martin-in-the-Fields had more than one origin. That there was a problem with the buildings did not feature on the job description when I was appointed Vicar in 1995, but it took me three months before I was confident to find my way round the astonishingly complex site which is much bigger than meets the eye. The interior of St Martin's was dirty, gloomy and looked worn out. It desperately needed a coat of paint. Under the courtyard the nineteenth-century burial vaults were intensively used by the Social Care Unit working with people who were mostly street homeless, as well as for a music rehearsal room, parish hall, Chinese People's Day Centre and some rather grim toilets. These vaults were dank, dark, airless and inaccessible. They leaked from above and flooded from below. No one complained about them – they were a given. Created as 'state of the art' care for the dead in 1828 they had been condemned in 1853 but used by the living throughout the twentieth century.

My predecessor, Geoffrey Brown, had done a very good job. He had extended the ministry of St Martin's in commercial terms and the business was making a significant contribution to church funds. This experiment in wealth creation and the church's engagement with the world of work had raised the game of St Martin's as a whole. Music was on the up, visitors had increased and the congregation had grown a little, particularly attracting younger professionals. On the down side the buildings just didn't add up and the Electoral Roll of 280 members was small for the amount of work that was being undertaken.

In the early summer of 1996 we held a congregational consultation. It was attended by about 100 people who answered two questions: Why do you come here? and What would you change? Overwhelmingly their response was that they came to St Martin's because they liked it and they wouldn't change anything. Yet, as for Geoffrey Brown, it was clear to me that trying to maintain the *status quo* was not an option. Looking back, much of the work at that early stage was 'capacity building' for the organizations making up St Martin's, but it took several years for us to begin to understand the complex problem of our buildings.

Location, location, location

In December 1997 Sir Peter Hunt, the Chairman and Chief Executive of our neighbours, Land Securities, died unexpectedly. It was a traumatic event for the firm, one of London's most respected property developers. His successor, Ian Henderson, asked to meet me so that we could plan a memorial service. On the morning of the service Ian's own father died, but only a handful of people in the church knew. He wanted to do what we had planned for Peter Hunt and afterwards go home to his family and more private grief. In such moments deep relationships are formed, and our partnership of ten years has been one of the keys to the renewal of St Martin's.

At that service, Clive Lewis said that 'Peter was not a great churchman but he would have loved this service. Every site we ever went to he said, "Location, location, location".' In gratitude and in memory of Sir Peter, Land Securities wanted to make a gift to St Martin's. I asked for a new grand piano as ours was over 60 years old and substandard for one of London's great concert rooms. They thought something for the Social Care Unit might be more appropriate and sent a small team to look at the accommodation in the vaults. They were shocked by what they saw and concluded that we only remained open because of the tolerant good will of Westminster City Council. Whatever could be done in memory of their former chairman in that context would have been like pouring water into a sieve.

At about the same time, the church had begun to think about what was needed to improve its appearance. A new conservation architect has been appointed to advise on the options for the church, crypt and vaults under the courtyard. A proposal was sketched to redecorate the church and improve access to the parish vaults not occupied by the Social Care Unit. An indicative cost of £3–5 million was given. It did not take long to realize that this, too, would have been like pouring water into a sieve. At best it would have been a cosmetic makeover and within a few years we would have wondered why we had wasted the opportunity.

Led by a churchwarden, Tricia Sibbons, the PCC asked the architects to think about the site, including the Social Care Unit. They produced a series of options for schemes with indicative costs of £8 million, £15 million and £22 million. Only the most expensive of these looked as though it would address the long-term problems of the site and equip St Martin's for service in the twenty-first century, but it included a narrow and unattractive new building in the eastern courtyard. Not surprisingly, English Heritage were less than enthusiastic about a new building impacting so negatively on one of London's landmarks. The London Diocesan Advisory Committee (DAC) told us we should consider the whole site, including the Nash terrace to the north which housed The London Connection, a project working with vulnerable young people in the West End. Their accommodation was the best in the St Martin's family, but without including it the DAC thought we would never unlock the potential of the whole site.

Ian Henderson stood in one of the old burial vaults that had been closed off because of damp, rubbing his eyes with disbelief that such an asset could sit unused on the edge of Trafalgar Square. He agreed to chair what we called the 'First Steps' group to help St Martin's raise sufficient money to form a plan, get planning permission and obtain a grant from the Heritage Lottery Fund. Ten years later, at the end of the project, he is still chairman, having had just a short break when the Project Development Board took over from the First Steppers before we formed the Development Trust and St Martin-in-the-Fields Building Renewal Project Limited. St Martin's would not have been renewed without him.

Beginning the relay race

When the PCC decided to go ahead with the project someone said in all seriousness, 'No one moves'. In fact it has been a relay race. I had assumed that one Project Director would see us through from beginning to end. Suzanna Lubran, who was appointed Project Director in 2001, described her skills as 'front end' and ran the first leg. Hugh Player then picked up the baton and has seen us through to the end. Suzanna suggested we publicly test the proposed scheme by taking it to the Commission for Architecture and the Built Environment for a critique. CABE were simply if ruthlessly brilliant. They concluded that we had demonstrated the need but had the wrong solution. They recommended we make a fresh start and gave us an 'enabling architect', Paul Williams of Stanhope Williams, to help us prepare a new brief and run an architectural selection competition.

We identified the internal and external stakeholders. Internally this was the five main organizations that made up St Martin-in-the-Fields. External agreement of the brief was secured from Westminster City Council, the London Diocesan Advisory Committee, English Heritage, the Georgian Group and the Prince's Foundation for the Built Environment. Because the project kept within this agreed brief and we continued to seek the help of these bodies, they remained supportive throughout, even when there were strong disagreements about detail.

The architectural competition attracted considerable interest. The selection panel was chaired by Charles Saumarez-Smith, then Director of the National Portrait Gallery across the road in St Martin's Place but successively Director of the National Gallery and now Secretary and Chief Executive of the Royal Academy of Arts. He has a passionate interest in architecture and had recently overseen the building of the NPG's highly acclaimed Ondaatje Wing. Another member of the panel, Sir William Whitfield, former Surveyor of the Fabric at St Paul's Cathedral and doyen of British architects, said the combination of heritage architecture, significance of the location and the complexity and intensity of use of the site made this the most challenging problem any of the architects being considered would face in their working lives.

Eric Parry's team produced the winning solution, modest in appearance but a radical reordering of the site with new spaces underground to a double depth of the existing vaults. Public attention focused on the new pavilion in Church Path. The Prince of Wales, Patron of the Development Trust, said that it must know its place in the urban setting between the great architecture of Gibbs and Nash. Nicholas Serota, Director of the Tate Gallery and a CABE Commissioner, said that it must be contemporary and speak of the early twenty-first century to later generations. It is a measure of the greatness of Eric Parry's scheme that both views have been satisfied, the glass pavilion being a contemporary material used in a classical architectural language.

The architectural team invested huge time and effort to understand the site and its many users. In talking to them we strengthened our own understanding of our purposes and of the relationships between the various parts of St Martin-in-the-Fields, which was a highly federal organization. As the scheme developed, Charles Saumarez-Smith observed that strong ideas often get diluted as they are worked out in practice, but the clarity of Eric Parry's initial proposal strengthened. The Project Team was assembled including Malcolm Reading Ltd, Gardiner and Theobald Associates, Alan Baxter Associates and Max Fordham Ltd.

Permissions were sought and obtained. The Chancellor of the Diocese of London presided over a Consistory Court in one of the old vaults under the courtyard with about 60 people present. For 17 minutes he listed all the representations he had received from statutory bodies and others before momentously concluding, 'There being no objections I rule in favour of the demolition of the vaults'. This was the first time English Heritage had not opposed the demolition of a listed building. They recognized the quality of the proposal, the careful restoration of the more important heritage architecture of the church and Nash terrace as well as the enhancement of its setting, and the significance of the working heritage of St Martin's that the new buildings would facilitate. Westminster City Council granted planning permission and have been unfailingly supportive. For the Diocesan Advisory Committee this was by far the largest and most significant project they have had to consider. They established a group to follow it closely and advise their whole committee in what has been an efficient and constructive process leading to the granting of faculties that permitted the work to go ahead with Diocesan approval.

'Unless the Lord builds the house . . .'

At the Sunday Eucharist on 5 January 2003 the Bishop of London, Richard Chartres, who has been a staunch supporter of the project, blessed the seven-volume application to the Heritage

Lottery Fund. Its success in securing a £15 million grant should have alerted other churches in the Diocese to the importance of this innovative liturgy, one of many used at each stage to pray the project into being. We have held vigils and prayed before Gift Days. St Martin's is not an especially wealthy community yet its members have given sacrificially and overall have contributed £1.8 million to this project, the largest gifts being legacies from those who died while we were making the journey.

Biblical passages gained significance at different stages of the project. Early on, when the going was tough I remember reading Psalm 127 repeatedly: 'Unless the Lord builds the house, those who build it labour in vain.' Verse 4 was chastening: 'It is vain that you hasten to rise up early and go so late to rest, eating the bread of toil, for he gives his beloved sleep.'

We all knew that the building work was going to be disruptive. The memory of how awful the vaults were carried us a long way without complaint. The community was up for the journey and there was very little complaining in the wilderness. The first phase finished were enabling works that removed the side chapel in church and created new toilets and a fire escape, allowing the church and Café in the Crypt to remain open through the first year of the project. We blessed the new toilets, cleanliness being next to Godliness, and told the congregation and staff that when they got despondent about all the work going on they should go to the toilet for an experience of the promised land.

Like the Israelites in the wilderness of Sinai, we struck the rock where the bore hole was to be drilled to see if the London aquifer 150 metres below would supply water to cool the new plant. It did. When the Bishop of New York presided over the ground-breaking ceremony at which there were also Jewish and Islamic blessings, the choir sang about Joshua at Jericho, 'and the walls came tumbling down' just as the vaults under the courtyard would be demolished. We have sent water cascading down the church steps and turned water into wine. We loved reading Ezra and Nehemiah about the building of the second temple in Jerusalem. The way they gathered resources with cedar from Lebanon encouraged us to gather the resources for the renewal of St Martin's from all over the world. Hong Kong has been marvellously supportive of our work with the Chinese. We have a US Foundation for St Martin-in-the-Fields London with its own small Board and the American Ambassador in London as Patron.

Never having done anything like this before, St Martin's grew what became a highly regarded and very effective small fundraising team led successively by Chris Phillips, Julia Chadwick and Barbara Davidson working with Patricia Castanha who continued to the end. People give to people and our advisers and network of friends and supporters were wonderfully effective on St Martin's behalf. What started with more than a degree of scepticism on the part of some whom we tried to involve, has become a reality.

'St Martin's on Tour'

John's Gospel, in which Jesus is glorified when raised up on the cross, spoke to us strongly during the disruption of early 2007 when the church was scaffolded before the period of closure. From May to September we became 'St Martin's on Tour'. Only our work with the most vulnerable, who turn to us for help through The Connection at St Martin's, remained on site. For nearly five months the rest of St Martin's was regularly on different sites across central London, including St Mary le Bow, St Giles in the Fields, St George's Bloomsbury, St Anne's Soho and St Paul's Covent Garden. There were three very special Evensongs at Lambeth Palace, the National Gallery and the Charterhouse and a wonderful parish weekend for over 80 people at Worth Abbey. There have been meetings at St Ethelburga's in Bishopsgate and in the temporary clergy flats in

Victoria. Concerts took place regularly at St Mary le Strand and St Mary le Bow as well as in the Banqueting House and National Portrait Gallery.

The welcome and hospitality we received was breathtaking. We lived by the kindness of friends. It was a pleasure to worship in each place, and their very varied witness was an encouragement and deepened our appreciation of London's Christian life. We felt better about being part of the Church of England than we had done for years. Paradoxically, the building project taught us about having no building of our own and being a pilgrim people.

Securing the future uncovered the past

In August 2006, as part of the buildings renewal, archaeologists from the Museum of London uncovered a Roman sarcophagus in a small area previously undisturbed by building works at the St Martin's Place end of the courtyard adjacent to Trafalgar Square. The skeleton inside was of a man in his mid-40s. He was 5′6″ tall and died in about the year 410, the year Rome fell and the army was recalled from Britain. He was almost certainly a contemporary of St Martin who died in the year 397 on the banks of the River Loire in northern France.

In an adjacent area the archaeologists also found some early Anglo-Saxon burials. They had previously thought that Roman Londinium and Anglo-Saxon Ludenwic did not overlap geographically. Here was unexpected evidence that they did. For St Martin-in-the-Fields the excitement was that these finds showed the site of the church to have been a sacred site from the early fifth century.

Peter Ackroyd, the novelist and author of *London: The Biography* said he thought it likely that the presence of a hot spring high above the River Thames would very early have established the site that is now St Martin's as a sacred site. The Roman sarcophagus was buried almost on an east–west axis, as is the custom with Christians, facing the rising sun and the new dawn of Christ's resurrection. At that time it is more likely than not that a person of high social status, as is implied by this large and expensive stone coffin, would have been a Christian but there is no proof. It was very much in keeping with the traditions associated with St Martin that pagan shrines were Christianized, and it is tempting to speculate that this is what happened on what is now the edge of Trafalgar Square.

Restored, renewed, reopened

On Sunday 30 September 2007 a congregation of nearly 500 gathered outside St Martin's. In the open air we read the beginning of the Passion Gospel according to Matthew, about a woman taking a jar of precious ointment and anointing Jesus. The Archbishop of Mexico anointed the doors and we followed the Easter Candle into the renewed church: 'The light of Christ: thanks be to God.' It was a great moment – the church restored, renewed and reopened. Having anointed the building we anointed one another: 'like living stones, let yourselves be built into a spiritual house, to be a holy priesthood, to offer spiritual sacrifices acceptable to God' (1 Peter 2.5).

There has been a strong spirit about this project. It had begun to renew us as a church even before the work on the buildings began. It has strengthened our local mission and ministry as well as our international links. When we halved our international missionary and charitable giving because of the project, unexpected and unsought-for gifts from individuals more than made up the reduction. They showed the importance of St Martin's as a conduit for funds to help others.

Several of the regular congregation have said how encouraged they have been that there has been such steady progress and so few difficulties. There is always more than one story, and those involved with the First Steps group, the Project Development Board, the Development Trust and Building Renewal Project Limited might tell it differently. On my reckoning there have been at least five occasions when the project nearly came off the rails. We have been saved by the sheer determination of the people committed to this project, miraculous unforeseen generosity and what seemed even to agnostics as 'acts of God'.

There were some marvellous moments, as when the Chair of the Heritage Lottery Fund put her hand on my shoulder and told me that what was needed was more prayer; and when one of our key supporters produced a cheque for £1 million from his back pocket as the necessary underwriting to secure agreement from the Heritage Lottery Fund to our beginning work even though not all the money was raised.

What has been achieved?

Even people who know the church quite well now struggle to remember how it looked before the renewal. The simple decorative scheme, close to its original, is light and beautiful, making the architecture even more striking. The first time I entered with Eric Parry after the reopening he said that one of his teachers had done his research on the significance of the circle in the Baroque. Look up at the ceiling above the galleries and you can see what this might have been about. The pulpit has moved to the north side, nearer its original position, opening up the sight-lines to the whole of the east end. The Victorian chancel and heavy fixed choir stalls have been replaced by Purbeck stone all on one level, with new furniture that can be moved to create a variety of flexible spaces in front of the restored line of the Georgian sanctuary. The side altar, introduced by Dick Sheppard in the 1920s has gone, and the woodwork throughout has been lovingly repaired and restored.

The windows are now of clear glass, as originally. A new east window has been installed, its strong horizontal and vertical lines making a cross which tightens at the centre around an ellipse of light, creation, and, to my mind, resurrection of an agony transformed. Such a prominent work by an Iranian artist, Shirazeh Houshiary, in a Christian church in the heart of London will focus the prayers of many for years to come. It is one of several arts commissions in keeping with the desire of those who built the church in the 1720s to give the best that London can offer to God. In our day we want to recover that eighteenth-century care for the aesthetic with the practical ethical tradition so characteristic of St Martin's in the twentieth century.

The eighteenth-century crypt under the church has been restored as a single volume and is a welcoming and hospitable Café in the Crypt. The new spaces under the courtyard are a sequence of practical and beautiful rooms that transform the possibilities of what we can do. They have been organized around the entrance pavilion and the light-well. A large foyer receives people and leads to St Martin's Hall, the Bishop Ho Ming Wah Chinese Centre and Dick Sheppard Chapel. There are three education and meeting rooms, named after people associated with St Martin's who continue to inspire us: Peter Benenson, the founder of Amnesty International; Florence Li Tim Oi, the first Anglican woman priest ordained in Macau on 24 January 1944; and Archbishop Desmond Tutu, anti-apartheid campaigner and a winner of the Nobel Peace Prize. Behind them, the Neville Marriner Room provides a music rehearsal room with associated changing rooms and offices to support what is one of London's major classical music venues as well as a church.

The church has been cleaned and its stonework extensively repaired, reminding us that when it was built it was known as the 'white church'. It has a new roof and its setting has been greatly improved by the realignment of the railings and widening of Church Path. The courtyard has become a quiet reflective space above the busy street. The Connection at St Martin's has been rehoused in purpose-built new spaces in the old school building and underneath the whole of the Nash terrace to the north of the site. It is a building that declares respect while also inviting purposeful change from those who come there seeking help. A new, narrow addition along almost the whole terrace joins up St Martin's behind the scenes, with separate outward faces.

A great team

The renewal of St Martin's has involved thousands of people. At its peak there were 240 workers on the building site, the tip of an iceberg of manufacturers, engineers and professional advisers. The pride they have taken in their work shows in every aspect of the project and will shine through for years to come. Geoff Hunt, Project Manager for Costain's the builders, and Paul Barker, St Martin's Project Manager from Gardiner and Theobald, have impressed in their management of such a complex undertaking.

One of the most moving things about the renewal project has been people's willingness to get involved. The Development Trust, with the Prince of Wales as Patron, was chaired by Ian Henderson and St Martin's Building Renewal Project Limited by John Anderson. We depended heavily on them and the other members of those Boards, senior people, all of them volunteers, who worked incredibly hard. They provided much expertise and support. A team of Campaign Advisers helped steer our fundraising, supported by other friends without any formal recognition but who played crucial roles. Sir Nicholas Goodison chairs our Arts Advisory Panel whose work will continue for several years beyond the renewal project.

Our existing internal Boards, St Martin-in-the-Fields Limited chaired by John O'Brien, The Connection at St Martin's chaired by Lady Diana Brittan with Colin Glover its Chief Executive, the Bishop Ho Ming Wah Chinese Centre chaired by Alastair Anson, and the Christmas Appeal chaired by Simon Wethered, kept the work of St Martin's going throughout: no small achievement. The Parochial Church Council has overseen a remarkable period of change with determination, courage and faith. The churchwardens Tricia Sibbons and Jane Whitley then Jeff Claxton and Andrew Caspari, and treasurers William Perraudin then Matthew Whalley, my Associate Vicars, successively David Monteith, Rosemary Lain-Priestley and Liz Griffiths with Paul Lau for the Chinese, and our Chief Executive, Hugh Player, have walked more than the extra mile many times. Indeed all the staff, church members and the wider St Martin's community have worked together to great effect for the renewal of St Martin's.

None of this work would have been possible without the thousands of donors who have paid for the renewal. Four gave £1 million or more, most gave much less – but all gave generously and at the top end of their ability to do so. A group of women in Soweto gave £60 in thanksgiving that one of their sons had been baptized at St Martin's in the 1980s during their years of exile from South Africa. This was not the standard pattern of fundraising campaigns, not least because the principal grant was from the Heritage Lottery Fund and the next largest from the Department for Communities and Local Government. So almost 50 per cent of the funding came from public sources, with the immense satisfaction that this reflects the public affection in which St Martin's is still held.

All that remains is for us to look forward, not back, and learn to use the new spaces for the common good in service of humanity and the greater glory of God. This is very much the way of St Martin's, so we can be confident about the future.

CHAPTER 10

Prayer for the day

The first-ever broadcast of a church service came from St Martin-in-the-Fields on 6 January 1924, the Feast of the Epiphany. As with so much about Dick Sheppard, the Vicar, the timing was impeccable. Here was the church making Christ known to the wider world, which is the purpose of Matthew's story of the magi bringing their gifts to the Christ child.

Sheppard thought the first radio service should have come from either St Paul's Cathedral or Westminster Abbey, but it is difficult for us to imagine how controversial this would have been. Not long before, someone had made a speech in the Church Assembly in which they said it would not be right to broadcast worship because you wouldn't know where people might listen to it. They might be in a public house, with their hats on. In response to that first broadcast Dick Sheppard received a letter from someone who had listened to it in a pub in Lewisham in south London where the men sang the hymns they had not sung since childhood and discussed the sermon over their pints of beer.

St Martin's has broadcast regularly ever since. With Bush House along the Strand, we were mostly World Service, while All Souls Langham Place, next to Broadcasting House in Portland Place, was Home Service. Nowadays St Martin's can be heard most often on BBC Radio 4 where I am one of the contributors to *Prayer for the Day*. It is broadcast so early (5.43 a.m.) that I used to assume only God listens, but now I know from emails and letters that there is an audience of insomniacs and larks.

The end of a book about ministry and renewal is, of course, not really an end but the start of a new day in the life of St Martin's. So a prayer about the renewal, which was broadcast in October 2007 just after we had come back into the renewed church, makes an appropriate end to *A Room with a View*. The hymn by George Herbert which it quotes is a piece of classical Anglicanism. This prayer points to wider horizons, which is exactly what those of us who have been involved in the renewal of St Martin's aspired to do.

A man that looks on glass

I haven't got used to going into church since the builders have been in. It's not just that St Martin-in-the-Fields, that much loved but dirty London church, has had a coat of paint and now looks clean. What seems to have made the biggest difference is that the coloured glass that was put in at the end of the war has been replaced by clear glass, like the Georgian original. Even with the scaffolding still up on the outside of the building, it lets in so much more light and makes the building dance, especially in the early morning.

And what I am looking forward to once the external scaffolding has come down is the visual connectedness of what happens inside the church with what's going on outside. Being able to see through the glass, above street level, should help us to pray the needs of the city around us.

The priest and poet George Herbert wrote what has become a favourite hymn: 'Teach me my God and King, in all things thee to see'. The verse that strikes me this morning is:

> A man that looks on glass,
>   On it may stay his eye;
> Or if he pleaseth, through it pass,
>   And then the heaven espy.

Glass separates an inner from an outer world. It reveals that
there is a reality beyond the limited horizons of the present, a
larger beyond from which light breaks in and gives a glimpse of
eternity.

> Lord God, may we delight in the rooms and buildings
>   that set our horizons.
> May we learn to live together creatively
>   in the limits of time and space,
> illumined by the light that comes from beyond
>   in which we glimpse eternity.
>
>   Amen

Notes

Chapter 1

1 Quoted in Joan Chittister, *In the Heart of the Temple: My Spiritual Vision for Today's World*, London: SPCK, 2005, p. 43.

2 For an analysis of this process, see Bruce Reed, *The Dynamics of Religion*, London: Darton, Longman and Todd, 1978.

3 Dick Sheppard, quoted in Malcolm Johnson, *St Martin-in-the-Fields*, Chichester: Phillimore, 2005, p. 47.

4 Bob Jackson, 'A Capital Idea', on the Diocese of London's website: www.london.anglican.org/CapitalIdea.

5 John Hull, in a critique of *A Mission-Shaped Church*, London: SCM, 2006.

6 The Lambeth Commission on Communion, *The Windsor Report*, London: Church House Publishing, 2004.

7 H. R. L. Sheppard, *The Impatience of a Parson*, London: Hodder and Stoughton, 1927.

8 David Paton, *RO – The Life and Times of Bishop Hall of Hong Kong*, Hong Kong: Diocese of Hong Kong and Macau, 1985, pp. 125ff.

9 David Beetge, 'The Future of the Anglican Communion', a lecture given at St Martin-in-the-Fields on 28 February 2005. It has been printed in *Christianity and Homosexuality: A Resource Booklet for Discussion*. Copies available from the Parish Secretary, 6 St Martin's Place, London WC2N 4JJ, price £3 inc. post and packing.

10 Nicholas Holtam and Sue Mayo, *Learning from the Conflict*, The Jubilee Group, 1998.

11 Douglas Board, *The Naked Year*, St Martin-in-the-Fields, 2004.

12 Danielle Hervieu-Leger, *Religion as a Chain of Memory*, Cambridge: Polity, 2000.

13 Archbishop's Commission on Urban Priority Areas, *Faith in the*

City: A Call for Action by Church and Nation, London: Church House Publishing, 1985.

14 Paul Avis, *A Church Drawing Near: Spirituality and Mission in a Post-Christian Culture*, T & T Clark, 2003, p. ix.

15 Simon Jenkins, *England's Thousand Best Churches*, London: Allen Lane, 1999, p. vii.

Chapter 2

1 P. Toynbee, *Hard Work: Life in Low-Pay Britain*, London: Bloomsbury, 2003.

Chapter 3

1 *Guardian*, Thursday 29 September 2005.

2 Rowan Williams, *Writing in the Dust: After September 11*, Grand Rapids, MI: Eerdmans, 2002.

3 Eamon Duffy, *Walking to Emmaus*, Burns & Oates, 2006.

4 Richard Dawkins, *The God Delusion*, London: Bantam Press, 2006.

5 *London Review of Books*, 19 October 2006.

6 Richard Dawkins, *The Selfish Gene*, Oxford: Oxford University Press, 1989.

7 Jim Wallis, *God's Politics*, London: HarperCollins, 2005.

8 Iris Murdoch, 'Vision and Choice in Morality', in I. T. Ramsey (ed.), *Christian Ethics and Contemporary Philosophy*, London: SCM, 1966.

9 C. Day-Lewis (1904–72), courtesy of Jill Balcon.

Chapter 4

1 Arundhati Roy, *The God of Small Things*, London: HarperCollins, 1997.

2 Albert Schweitzer, *The Quest of the Historical Jesus*, London; SCM Press, 2000 (1909).

Chapter 5

1 *The National Gallery Companion Guide*, London: The National Gallery.

2 Michael D. Goulder, *Midrash and Lection in Matthew*, London: SPCK, 1974.
3 *The National Gallery Companion Guide.*

Chapter 6
1 Kenneth Kirk, *The Vision of God*, Cambridge: James Clarke and Co., 1991.
2 David Goodman, *Fault Lines: Journeys into the New South Africa*, Berkeley: University of California Press, 1999.
3 Lynn Lavner, *A Collection of Quotable Quotes*, Advanced Marketing (UK) Ltd, 2004.
4 Lionel Blue, *To Heaven with Scribes and Pharisees*, London: Darton, Longman and Todd, 1975.

Chapter 7
1 Reinhold Niebuhr, *Moral Man, Immoral Society*, Westminster John Knox Press, 2002.
2 Ken Leech, *The Long Exile*, London: Darton, Longman and Todd, 2001, p. 113.
3 Kirk, *The Vision of God*, Cambridge: James Clarke and Co., 1991.